Mikhail Berkut was born in Od
the siege of Stalingrad with h
whilst his father was killed in a

Following a master's (
choreography at Moscow The
worked throughout the former Soviet Union.

After emigrating from the USSR, Mikhail settled in Canada, where he founded "Les Ballets Russes de Montreal" and the character dance company "Kalinka". His sixty-year creative career spanned Western Europe, culminating in the UK at The Royal Ballet School and Doreen Bird College. He has published several books and videos on dance.

(*Left to right*) Mikhail, aged 13; Anna, Mikhail's mother, aged 42; Roman, aged nine; Iosif, aged 15.

Beam of Hope

MIKHAIL BERKUT

Beam of Hope

Vanguard Press

VANGUARD PAPERBACK

© Copyright 2015
Mikhail Berkut

Cover image courtesy of
Bundesarchiv, Bild 183-B22176 / CC-BY-SA

A CIP catalogue record for this title is
available from the British Library.

ISBN 978 178465 019 3

Vanguard Press is an imprint of
Pegasus Elliot Mackenzie Publishers Ltd.
www.pegasuspublishers.com

First Published in 2015

Vanguard Press
Sheraton House Castle Park
Cambridge England

Printed & Bound in Great Britain

Beam of Hope is an ode to my mother,
and wholly dedicated to her.

Acknowledgements

My heartfelt thanks and gratitude are due to Andrew Winstone for his invaluable assistance in improving the English text of my book whilst preserving the character of its content.

My thanks also go to Judy Perraton for her part in the project.

Contents

Chapter 1

OVERTURE TO WAR

"Mummy! Time to go to the beach! *Muummy*! Can you hear me? Bother. Hey, dogface – what's the big mystery? Our parents have been talking in there for ages."

"Listen, plinkety-plonker, call me that again and I'll whack you so hard, even Mother won't recognise you!"

"All right, dogface, put that book down and let's go for a swim."

A heavy volume violently struck the back of my head, pre-empting my retaliation. The red mist descended and yet again, my older brother and I were rolling around on the floor in a tight clinch, destroying everything in our path. I managed to sink my teeth into his hand, and he screamed. Hearing the kerfuffle, our father threw open the door and rushed into the room. He picked us up off the floor, separated us by the scruff of our necks, and shook us.

"What are you fighting about this time? Shame on you both! You don't give the neighbours downstairs a moment's peace, with your constant squabbling."

"Semyon, your nerves," my mother intervened. "Let me deal with these two."

"S'not my fault!" yelled Yosif. "Look! He bit me and drew blood!"

"That's because he bashed me so hard on the head with *Robinson Crusoe* he nearly killed me!" I whimpered, relying on my parents' customary soft spot for the younger child. As usual, it paid off.

"Yosif, you're eleven years old," Mother said sternly to my elder brother. "It's about time you behaved like it."

Father tried to even things out. "And you, Misha darling, must have more respect for your brother – he's two years older than you."

"He's *not* two years older than me," I protested. "Only a year and nine months!"

"In any case," Mother added categorically, "You must stop your silly squabbling from now on, because something dreadful happened this morning – not just for our family, but for the entire Soviet nation."

Her voice faltered. She turned away and went to the bedroom, where three-year-old Roman was now awake. My brother and I stood bewildered, open-mouthed. Father sat on the edge of the chair, pulled us towards him and sighed heavily, his head low.

"I realise that you children are too young to understand what war is about..."

"I know," the eldest interrupted. "It's when Red Indians fight white people, or pirates rob the rich!"

Father shook his head. "Unfortunately, lads, this is a totally different kind of war. There's nothing in the least romantic about it. I'm sure you've heard at school that there's been a world war in Europe these past two years…"

"Oh, yes," Yosif volunteered. "Our teacher told us that Germany won't go to war with us now that Hitler and Stalin have signed the peace treaty."

How come he knew all that? Although annoyed, I held my tongue. Only one class ahead of me, and just look at him showing off like a know-all. I'll make him pay for that…

"By the way, Daddy, why does Germany have to go to war with us? What's in it for them?"

"Stupid!" Yosif shouted. "They'll capture us all and make us slaves."

"Stupid yourself!" I snarled back. "You just think you're above everyone else because you've read all those fantasy adventure stories."

I had overheard Mother tell him off about this in the kitchen, and memorised the criticism in case it would come in useful. He opened his mouth, ready to nail me, but a gesture from father put a stop to our squabbling.

"Boys, as of this morning, we are at war. The Nazis have attacked us. Everyone in the country is urgently being mobilised by the Red Army to fight for our nation's freedom. The announcement is being broadcast on every radio station. I'll also be leaving for the front in a few days, to protect our beloved Odessa from the enemy."

I felt a sudden lump in my throat. I could hear Mother crying in the bedroom, where little Roman was desperately offering her his toys in an attempt to comfort her. Yosif, stunned, stared at father. After a long pause, he took a deep breath, and continued.

"This is the first time in this family we've talked man-to-man, and I hope you'll take it seriously. War is not about rolling around on the floor, biting each other like puppies (I felt my cheeks flush). Soldiers fight to the death, to defend themselves, our country and our freedom. You, too, will have trials to face. Unless we stop the advance of the enemy immediately, you and Mummy will have to leave Odessa for a while and go inland. After our victory, I'll come and find you, wherever you are, and we'll all come back together to our wonderful city. I give you my word, as your father. However, you must promise me to obey your mother without question, to help her in every way, to protect each other from any trouble or mishaps, and to stick together at all times."

"Semyon, don't frighten the children," urged Mother anxiously as she walked up behind him. She grabbed our heads, and pressed them against her, almost convulsively. "They're too young to know about war and death..."

"Annushka, please! Stop being hysterical. From now on, they're no longer children. They're young fighters who will protect our family. No more baby talk. They must let go of your apron strings to be ready to face the troubles ahead. I have faith in our sons' future. They will survive the hard times ahead, I'm sure."

Father spoke in the same portentous tone as the radio presenter announcing the outbreak of war. With a heavy step, he went to the bedroom to entertain whimpering little Roman. We both stood there, unable to speak, feeling confused and bereft. Our heads were bathed with Mother's tears as she held us close, as if to protect us from the disaster to come.

From 22nd June 1941, during the first month of the war, life in Odessa was hard, as it was in the rest of the country. Despite the hot summer, the beaches were deserted. Long queues formed in the shops, and the streets were animated by a kind of muted bustle, like a silent movie. Many relatives from all walks of life came to our house. During the day, women would come to ask Mother's advice on how best to keep their children safe, and shared food and medicine. In the evening, after work or military training, came the men who were not yet at the front, to discuss when and how to evacuate their families, or the safety or otherwise of those of Jewish origin, as opposed to those of the faith, in the occupied territories. Our father categorically insisted on the evacuation of all our relatives, but some of his brothers and sisters were reluctant to part with their possessions, and hoped for commercial cooperation with the Nazis. In the end, they paid for their greed with the lives of their entire families, which was especially heart-breaking because of the children.

In mid-July 1941, my father was dispatched to the front line of Odessa's defences. Before leaving, he warned

Mother about the evacuation due to take place a week later. Frantic preparations were made for our departure. We had never seen Mother so serious or so implacably organised. None of us knew when or where we were going, or how long we would be away. On the night of the 21st–22nd of June, our city suffered its first bombing raid. There were sirens, explosions, and mills and factories ablaze. In the morning, we were picked up by a large cart drawn by two horses. Mother helped the driver to load our bundles and suitcases, perching all three children on top. She replied calmly to the questions of astonished neighbours, and promised to be back in a month, after the victory. Who could have guessed that victory would take another four years? For us children, the horse-drawn journey seemed an exotic start to the school holidays. Mother sat next to the driver, and we set off on a trip that was to prove longer and more dramatic than we had anticipated in Odessa. Something inside me said farewell to my childhood.

At the military checkpoint at the city gates, our very own commander-in-chief showed the officer her documents, and they let us go with a warning that, sooner or later, our horses would be requisitioned for the war effort. The driver opted to take small country roads. In every village, we were greeted with curiosity and kindness; we were the first war refugees in that district, as it turned out. Kind-hearted women gave us generous amounts of fruit, milk and other food. Although the harvest had been exceptionally plentiful in the Ukraine that year, there had been no one to gather it in. Vegetables and cereals withered and rotted in the fields.

Our driver, a peasant, wiped his tears with his sleeve as we drove past yet another agricultural graveyard. Far behind us, vivid tableaux of glades, clearings and lakes were being destroyed by the ravages of war. Yet here, paradoxically, we felt as though everything was oddly at peace in the beautiful harmony of nature – cruel irony, a malevolent joke at the expense of the creator.

All day, the driver only stopped to allow passengers to relieve themselves in the bushes, or to water the horses. We ate as we went. He tried to put as much distance as possible between us and the front line. I sometimes chased after the cart, leaping onto the back as it rumbled along, whistling as I dangled my feet before hopping off again to run barefoot on the dusty road. Mother denied Yosif this fun and games because of his 'heart problem' that the doctor had apparently diagnosed. I, on the other hand, had run errands for milk and bread from an early age. I was proud of Mother's faith in me, but I sometimes thought that my older brother sneered maliciously at my enthusiasm. He was constantly asserting his superiority and looked on me as a naive idiot. He treated little Roman like a complete nobody, and was often jealous of our mother's attentions towards him – she hardly ever let the youngest out of her arms. I was rather proud of being nicknamed 'the Golden Middle' by our relatives for my musical abilities. At the age of five, I had begun studying the violin at music school, and moved to the piano department a year later. I was quick at picking up popular tunes and playing them by ear, and even tried singing them to my own accompaniment. War, however, interrupted all this easy success. Both the music school and my street playmates vanished into the distance, like a wonderful dream. All we were left with was the noisy reality of the monotonously squeaking wheels of the cart, the driver urging on the horses and the burning sun over our heads.

After travelling for four days, we reached Dnepr. As we were about to cross the river, we were stopped at the bridge by a military patrol. The soldiers fumbled for a long time with Mother's documents, talked to the driver, then asked us to wait while they called their superior. Eventually, he emerged and explained to Mother that we could proceed no further because our horses and cart were being requisitioned for the war effort. We were driven over the bridge to the outpost on the other side of the river, our luggage was unloaded inside the precinct, and we were supposed to wait until the authorities decided what to do with us refugees. Our driver returned with a piece of paper in lieu of our horses. Mother handed him an envelope which I guessed contained money. He gave us a look of pity, furtively crossed himself, and disappeared back over the bridge.

"You two, wait here," Mother ordered, as she brushed bits of straw off her skirt, removed the dirty scarf from her head, and smoothed her hair. "I'm going with Roman now, to sort things out. Remember, don't under any circumstances leave our luggage unattended until I get back from the office (which was what she called the outpost).

She looked at my brother and me. "Do you understand?" We both nodded silently and sat on top of our bundles, spreading out our arms over the rest. I thought these must be the trials father had referred to in his instructions to us at the start of the war. Our commander grabbed Roman by the hand and headed for the outpost. As she reached the steps, the duty guard at the gate shouted after her, "Where are you going, woman?" but it was too late. Mother decisively opened the door, dragging Roman in after her. Our youngest was a little scared of all the stern-looking armed men in uniform, and reluctant to go near them. Later, we understood that she had taken him along deliberately, for noise value, which worked out a treat. The office window was open wide, so although we could not see anything, we heard every word of the exchange. Mother asked him what he intended to do with us, since we had no means of transport.

The officer interrupted his telephone conversation, and replied that we were free to do as we pleased. Mother seemed to have been waiting for just that, and she pounced like a panther. Her maternal instinct must have instructed her exactly how to act when threatened. She began screaming hysterically and ruthlessly went for the foolish officer's jugular. "You, a Soviet officer, leaving me with three young children to spend the night under a bridge, at the mercy of fate!" Roman began to wail.

Soldiers rushed in, awaiting orders. With the ferocity of Kipling's Bagheera, she persevered in her attack: "And you consider yourself a representative of the Red Army? Only Nazis would act this way! Take us to the nearest town or district centre immediately, while it's still daylight, or you'll have to answer to a tribunal for the way you're treating the family of a fighting soldier!"

There was no stopping her. The chief of the precinct seemed to have lost the power of speech. He went into the next door office and apparently telephoned someone, since telephone operators and nurses began to gather around. They all tried to comfort the mother in distress. Roman was screaming like a slaughterhouse piglet. My elder brother and I were also sobbing, but did not abandon our positions. The whole scenario was completely out of place in this precinct.

Suddenly, out of nowhere, a horse and cart appeared speeding over the bridge. It was the chairman of the nearest district coming in person at the request of the military authorities to settle the matter. He took us to his village on the spot, and organised for us to spend the night at the local farm cooperative centre. It was a warm welcome. We were fed, washed and put to bed. Even so, Mother spent a long time trying to consolidate our future security with this new protector. He was the mayor of the village, and promised to take us the next morning to nearby Zarnitza farm, where we could live for as long as we wished.

Worry prevented me from falling asleep for a long time. In the parlour, Mother was explaining to the chairman how we had ended up here, and how the bureaucratic senior officer had confiscated our means of transport and refused to help us. The old man tried to pacify her with his velvety voice, and attempted to justify the young officer's uncaring cruelty by his inexperience and the general panic created by being at war. Anna told him that our father was supposed to come for us in two or three weeks, but the mayor restrained her optimism. He informed her that the enemy was unfortunately fast advancing into the depths of the Ukraine, and that we would consequently have to stay longer. Mother fell silent, visibly upset. As for me, I felt as though I had just been cut down.

The landlady woke us up at daybreak. The chairman was already waiting for us outside, with transport. After a rushed breakfast of milk and fresh warm bread, we set off, full of suspicion and anxiety, for our new home. Although Mother put on a brave face, we sensed her anxiety from the questions she was asking the mayor: "How far is this farm? Where will we live, and at whose expense will we eat? Is there a telephone or telegraph line? Is there public transport into Zaporojye district centre?"

Our new protector answered all Mother's questions clearly and patiently. He even promised, if the worst came to the worst, to take us to Zaporojye town council himself, to join the evacuation. This kind-hearted man inspired trust with his calm tone and presence. After one bend in the road, he reined in the horse from a trot to a slower pace. A fairytale view unfolded before us: on our left, orchards where women were picking fruit; on our right, in the distance, a series of streams where boys were washing horses. Far ahead, like little jewels, a scattering of white huts against the lush greenery. We turned our heads in every direction, rendered speechless by this idyllic village landscape. At the sight of the chairman, the fruit pickers cried out warm greetings and waved. He responded by waving his straw hat above his head. As we discovered later, his sister lived alone in Zarnitza. She had her own house, garden, vegetable patch and animals. In the summer, her grandchildren came from the city to spend the holidays with her. This year, however, they had changed their plans because of the war.

The mayor brought us to her, knowing she wouldn't refuse refugees shelter. Mother, who had discovered all this on our way there, promised to help out around the house and in the kitchen, to repay the hospitality. Klava was a friendly, energetic peasant woman of seventy, with a kind heart. With the help of visiting children and her brother, her household was in good order. Mother befriended her immediately, and we settled in, warm and safe. Yosif spent most of his time reading in the book hut, while I made friends with the local children of my own age. Every day, our merry band would rush to bathe in the streams. My new friends taught me to ride, and every time I came tumbling off the horse, they fell about laughing – and so did the horse. For a long time, I walked all bow-legged and with a sore behind, but I endured it bravely and refused to admit defeat.

After lunch, when the heat subsided, Klava would show me how to pull out weeds and water the ripening vegetables, how to pick berries from thick bushes and collect fruit under the trees in the garden. At first I had backache from lack of practice, but the many new things I learnt in such a short time from this sweet and boundlessly energetic grandmother more than made up for it. Mother sometimes worried about my health. She had no inkling of the immense pride I felt when flaunting to Yosif my expertise in distinguishing harmful insects from edible ones, and knowing the different types of root vegetable.

"Who wants to dig around in dung, anyway?" was his reaction.

"But you're quick enough to stuff yourself with salad or borscht, aren't you?" I replied, having the final word before rushing back to the hen house, the pigsty or somewhere else equally exotic in the vicinity.

While Roman was at kindergarten, Mother cooked, washed, cleaned house and, every single day, went to the post and telegraph office to check if there was news from father. She returned frowning and obviously preoccupied. Klava confided in whispered tones that Hitler foamed at the mouth like a rabid dog, and burned down everything in his way. As soon as they saw us children playing in blissful ignorance, the women would fall silent. Still, we could sense an end to the carefree holiday approaching, knowing our luck could not last. It was obvious that new tribulations awaited us around the corner. One evening at the end of our third week in Zarnitza, the telephone operator came from the post office to tell Mother that we had to get ready to leave immediately, and that the chairman himself would come for us early in the morning. "Here we go again," I muttered unhelpfully.

We quickly packed our few belongings and went to bed. Mother stayed up, busying herself in the kitchen and the parlour. She washed, cleared and cleaned every last speck of dust, not to leave any dirt behind us in the house. Not for nothing did our relatives in Odessa call her a cleanliness fanatic. As I drifted to sleep, I could hear Klava through the wall, in the bedroom next to mine, praying in despair as she repeated "Holy Mother of God, have mercy upon us." Once, I noticed her hiding an icon under her old mattress. I longed to see the image on it, but was too shy to ask. Father used to tell us, "You must always restrain your curiosity if you don't want to attract misfortune or get into trouble." What did he mean, though? My touching other people's things with dirty hands? So should I wash my hands before handling other people's belongings? The whole thing seemed strange.

Before dawn, we loaded the now familiar cart. Our kind protector Andrei Petrovitch kept urging us to hurry, as the journey before us was long – five hours to

Zaporojye, where we had to catch the evacuation train to Lugansk. Klava handed Mother a bag of food, a can of water and two bottles of milk. Hiding behind her brother, she quickly made the sign of the cross over us, holding back her tears. As a mark of gratitude for everything, our mother offered our silver cutlery wrapped in a tea towel as a gift, which Klava vehemently declined. I was so sad about leaving this kind old woman that I jumped off the cart, ran to hug her, and head butted her in the belly. She kissed me on the head, put me back on my seat, and said, "God be with you, Annushka!" The mayor cracked the reins, and we were off again towards an uncertain future, but which was to take us closer to the front line.

As usual, Mother travelled next to the driver. I sat on the bags, with my back to them. Yosif and Roman were on the main seat, facing in the direction of travel. I wanted to keep Zarnitza in view for as long as I could, as it slowly vanished into the distance, and to say goodbye forever to something which had become an indistinguishable part of me after such a short time. The red orb of the sun was only just rising from behind the horizon. Housewives were chasing cattle out of their homes. Cows were lowing their greetings to one another, and gathering at the back of the farm. With his stick, the old stockman was prodding them towards the streams, where they would graze in their own vast meadows for the rest of the day. Once we had rounded the bend in the road, everything vanished as though a curtain had fallen on it, and I began listening in to the conversation behind me.

"The Germans are bombing Dnepropetrovsk. It's a military target, like the other industrial centres. We won't be able to keep the enemy back for much longer."

Mother was frightened. "But that's so near – we must catch the train at all costs!" she exclaimed. Then, as though suddenly remembering herself, she dropped her voice back down to a whisper. "Tell me honestly, is this really the last evacuation train? I need to know what the situation is for the children and me. You know what the Nazis will do to us if we get stuck in Zaporojye!"

"Don't worry yet, Anna. I'll do everything in my power to send you and the children deep inland."

"Thank you so much for your help. You're our only hope."

"You needn't thank me. It's an honour for me to ensure that your family is safe. But for my plan to succeed, I need you to stay calm and trust me."

"I promise," Mother replied. "Only please tell me your plan, so I can feel a bit more at ease."

"Well, my daughter works as a dispatcher at the goods train station. In an hour, when we reach my village, I'll phone her from my office and ask her for help. She won't refuse."

At that moment, Roman woke up from dozing, and asked to get some air. Mother asked to stop and all three of us, bladders bursting, walked into a sunflower plantation. It was the first time we had seen how the seeds grew. Before the war, father had spent years working in a factory that extracted sunflower seed oil, and crushed the shells to a pulp for horses, pigs and cattle. I asked the chairman's permission to pick three sunflower heads, and we distracted ourselves by nibbling on the seeds like squirrels for the rest of the journey.

We stopped for a break at the district centre. While the mayor was phoning from his office, we had lunch in the buffet, and lay on the grass of the municipal garden. At the same time, a woman from the district council fed and watered our horse, chatting with Mother about something or other. I perked up my ears, expecting to hear news.

"Any news, Andrei Petrovitch?" our leader asked impatiently.

"My daughter promised to check the timetable of trains going east, and asked me to call her again when we get nearer the town."

"And what about the evacuation of local people further inland?"

"She doesn't know exactly because in the last three days, all the trains have been dispatched as and when, without following an exact timetable."

We spent the remaining two hour journey in tense silence. Andrei Petrovitch kept urging the horse on, and glancing at his watch. In the distance, ahead of us, the outskirts of Zaporojye became visible. We stopped at the suburban post office and the mayor called his daughter again. He took a long time, and when he finally returned, it was obvious to Anna, from the expression on his face, that our problems were not a priority.

His daughter said that the evacuation train was full to bursting with local refugees, and had therefore left an hour earlier. The remaining families with children had been taken to the station waiting room until tomorrow's train. When Mother tried to say something, he stopped her with his hand and announced that this would not be a problem for our family. They were going to try and make an exception for us, as a mother on her own with three children. It would therefore be better if she kept quiet and left the decision to the people whose job it was.

Mother consented, and we drove to the freight station. On the way, we were stopped several times by military patrols. Each time, Andrei Petrovitch showed his official government documents and they let us through. It was evening before we reached the marshalling yard. The mayor's daughter, Larissa, who was about Mother's age, was waiting for us. She and her father carried our belongings into an office, and told us to make ourselves comfortable in the armchairs and on the couch. Then they asked us to wait there and not go anywhere while they organised our departure that same night. Roman was misbehaving, Yosif was going on and on about the mayor and his daughter not coming back, while I insisted that a man like that would keep his word and never lie to us.

A couple of hours later, they did return. They sat at the desk with Mother, pencil and paper in hand. Andrei

Petrovitch began explaining the complicated situation, and writing down instructions, the names of the engine drivers, and the least dangerous route east.

"Unfortunately, there are no closed freight trains scheduled for tonight," Larissa said. "Dnepropetrovsk is under continual bombardment, and the same will start here any day now. There are open wagons carrying iron eastwards through Makeyevka. Both drivers – the engine was repaired in the depot here – will take you with them in their cabin until that junction, where they'll take on open wagons transporting iron to Lugansk this very night. We have no legal authority beyond that point. In the morning, as soon as you get there, you must go immediately to the local evacuation point, where they'll explain everything about refugee transportation onwards that the Lugansk authorities have organised. The only serious problem is the part from Makeyevka to Lugansk, which will take three or four hours. You'll have to travel in an open wagon with red ore, though it'll be secured by tarpaulin."

Mother listened without interrupting, her eyes growing wider. From the front line not far away, we could hear the roar of guns and, on the dark horizon, we could see the glow of flares or shells, confirming the approaching threat.

"Anna, are you listening? Don't get distracted," Andrei Petrovitch continued. "The engine drivers will help you in Makeyevka; they both have large families. The crushed ore will be like a mattress for you. They'll put you into one of the front carriages to keep an eye on you during the journey. These," he demonstrated, "are the straps for securing the tarpaulin to the walls of the wagon. Once the ore is loaded onto the carriage, it's arranged in a conical shape. Each one of you will be strapped, like a parachutist, to a bundle or a case, counterbalancing the other side of this cone, with a 10–20 cm gap between you and the belt. That way, you'll be able to turn around from one side to the other while the train is moving. Trains are fast at night, so your discomfort may not last as long as we think. My daughter and I fully appreciate that it's by no means the easiest way to save your children. But you don't have much choice. Either you stay at the passenger station with the other refugees, and wait for tomorrow's train, or set off with the engine drivers immediately. I'm afraid that's really all we can do for you. As a mother, Anna, it's entirely up to you."

Andrei Petrovitch stopped talking, and waited. Mother stared into his eyes for a long time, as though checking that his proposal was indeed real, and not some awful nightmare. Then she rose slowly, and said "Right – let's go!" – so we went to the station with our belongings. The drivers were already waiting for us at the buffet. They quickly picked up our things and led us over the rails to the locomotive. Mother carried Roman in her arms, while Larissa held my hand. Yosif walked alone behind us, showing off his independence. The locomotive was already standing by. The drivers skilfully tied our luggage to the hand rails and helped Yosif and me climb into their cabin while Mother said emotional goodbyes to the mayor, and his daughter gave last minute instructions to the drivers.

Finally, we were all cooped up in the small, sweltering cabin. Quietly at first, the locomotive started to move. Mother waved her scarf out of the window at our saviours for a long time, until they disappeared into the gloom. I sat on the floor in the corner, and thought this must the beginning of the second 'trial' father had foretold. One thing I could not understand, however was why had we embarked on such a risky a journey when we could have joined a large group of other evacuee families, like people did in other cities? It seemed that Mother had a blind faith in the radio broadcasts that assured us that we would soon beat the enemy, allowing us return to Odessa before long. Father had always been wise; I will never know what pushed him to take such a risk.

Anna sat on some sort of crate, with Roman asleep in her lap. My brother and I fidgeted in different corners of the floor, so the engine drivers kept having to step over us in order to move around. They communicated mostly by mime and gesture because of the loud rattling of the wheels and the engine. Fortunately, the train ran at full speed with few interruptions, save for the occasional stop at a junction to change points and replenish the water. Dozing fitfully, we only realised that we were approaching Makeyevska when we were woken by the calls of a military patrol asking about the things hanging from the external handrails. Our drivers told them the dramatic story of the family of a fighting soldier, and Mother produced a sheaf of documents which the young conscripts studied, torch in hand. They scrutinised every corner of the cabin, and even peeked into the burning furnace. Then they exchanged bewildered looks, and saluted us.

After that, everything proceeded according to plan. The drivers found their next train already waiting for them, fully loaded, and the local signalmen attached our locomotive to the open-top ore wagons. Before anything else, Mother dragged us behind the carriages to relieve ourselves, and the men's strong arms helped us climb on top of the loads, our feet pushing against the inside walls of the wagon. One of the drivers attached my brother and his large bag to the other side of the ore cone for balance, as had been planned in Zaporojye, while his colleague did the same with me, but with less of a counterbalance. Mother, watching from below, held her head in her hands with disbelief at what she was seeing. As if that was not enough, Roman, deprived of sleep, sat wailing loudly beside the rails.

By contrast, my brother and I both found it quite fun to be tied to our rucksack counterbalances. It all seemed unreal, like a cheap vaudeville act. Finally, the men heaved up Mother and Roman, tied them together at the waist in a hugging position to balance their combined weight against the suitcase. Once again, we checked that all the fastenings were within reach, and that the extensions could be stretched. As a precaution, the drivers made us wear our jackets and berets, even though it was a warm night. They explained that travelling at full speed in an open-top wagon would get chilly. Bright stars dotted the sky, and searchlight beams scanned the sky. An ominous, brooding silence had fallen over the blacked-out city. There was something mystical about it all.

After the drivers had once again checked that the wagons were securely linked, we were ready to embark upon the next part of our adventure. "Dear Father," I wrote in my head, "the cruel trials of the war continue." We were all so exhausted that, unsurprisingly, we soon fell asleep, lulled by the rhythmic sway of the train. Only Mother did not sleep; she kept a watchful eye on us, like the mother hen I saw in Klava's coop. The drivers took it in turns to climb into the wagon to check on us at regular intervals. When they called out, Mother would wave an 'all's well' gesture with her free arm. Later, she would always remember these men, so coarse and yet so full of natural kindness, sincerity and respect for a woman with three children. When we reached Lugansk, she practically had to force our selfless saviours to accept the family silver, as a token of our heartfelt gratitude for their patience and help.

"Mummy, teach told us that gold and silver are precious metals. So why are you giving away our things?"

Anna smiled at my attempt to be clever. "First of all, it's teacher, not 'teach'," she corrected. "And secondly, such treasures can sometimes cost people their lives."

I was surprised. "I don't understand."

"Idiot," my older brother began.

"You're the thick one!"

"You're still too little to understand," he went on, patronisingly. "If thieves find out we have silver, they'll want to steal it, see, and could even kill a little squirt like you for it."

"You – you're nothing but a... a sunflower!" I finally retaliated, failing to find a worthy riposte.

"And thirdly, Misha," Mother interrupted, "you must always be civil to people, especially kind strangers who've just saved you from harm."

And so there it was – another life lesson for me. A woman porter with a cart took our belongings to the evacuation point at the station, where the benches were occupied by families waiting for the train east. The porter took our documents to one of the windows, and returned to say that we'd be seen in half an hour. When Mother offered her a rouble in thanks, the woman beamed and asked if we wanted anything from the buffet (where all they had was buns and tea). Within a minute, the three of us were devouring stale buns, and scalding our tongues on hot, sugarless tea. Mother tried to remind us of good table manners but after a long sleepless night, we were much too hungry and crotchety for that. When the official called us in, Roman was fast asleep on top of our bundles, Yosif was re-reading Jules Verne for the tenth time and I was subjecting Mother to interminable 'why?' questions. She took me with her into the interview room to avoid any possible scrap between me and Yosif, who stayed to look after Roman and our belongings.

The supervisor turned out to be a sullen-looking woman, obviously weary of dealing with tiresome refugees. "Not all executive committee members have the kind of patience to deal with people who've just lost their normal way of life," thought Mother, readying herself for a fight with bureaucracy. After completing our registration papers, the supervisor announced that we had been added to the list of evacuees leaving at ten that evening on the train for Uzbekistan. Our commander suddenly sat up.

"Excuse me, but is that the only place you're sending people, or are there others?"

The supervisor was indignant. "Why don't you want to go to Tashkent?"

"Back in Odessa, my sisters and I agreed that we'd all wait for one another in Stalingrad, so we can all live together and help each other out..."

"You don't have a choice," the supervisor rudely interrupted. "You'll go wherever we decide to send you, and where other people like you are going. Here are your documents, your coupons for the trip and the food. Have a good trip."

We said goodbye and went back into the waiting room, stunned as if a bucket of cold water had just been thrown in our faces. I could feel Mother's hand shaking on my shoulder, either from anger or exhaustion. I didn't know how to help her, so I sat her down on the nearest bench and, as usual, began to pontificate.

"Anna Davidovna, you're always telling us that we should take a deep breath whenever we feel very sad." She pulled me to her and, for the first time ever as far as I could remember, she pressed my hand against her cheek. How long this blissful moment lasted, I don't know, but it was interrupted by the familiar voice of the woman porter.

"Madam, do you need any help?"

Anna opened her eyes. "No thank you. Or, actually – yes. My name's Anna – what's yours?"

"Darya. Why are you upset?"

My mother spoke quietly. "I need information and some help if you have time when you're not working."

"Don't worry about that, for God's sake. I've also got children and a soldier husband. How can I help?"

Mother explained our predicament, asked the time of the next train for Stalingrad, and if she knew of anyone interested in buying a pair of golden earrings cheaply. Darya listened, nodding; she thought a little, and then replied, "There's no direct train to Stalingrad on the timetable. Only two carriages – a communal one and another with compartments – which they attach to a train which stops every morning at eleven-thirty at a station not far from Lugansk."

"There's four of us, plus luggage, so we really need a separate compartment," said Mother.

The porter was clearly concerned. "Yes, but compartments are very expensive and, to be honest, they're not even for sale because they're reserved for authorities or important guests."

Mother had an idea. "Yes, but we're the family of a high official in Odessa."

Darya gave a calculating smile. "May I see the earrings?" she asked, curious. Rummaging in her handbag, Mother revealed a glimpse of her wedding present and produced a receipt showing the number of carats and a price of 750 roubles. "I'm prepared to sell them for half that in exchange for a private compartment and prepaid tickets all the way to Stalingrad," she stated firmly. "I'll also give you something to thank you if you manage to sort us out."

"I don't know what I can do. I need to speak to the woman on duty at the station. See – that one over there, in the red cap. We've been working together for fifteen years and often help each other out. After all the men went to war, we women all got closer, all of us 'friends in misfortune'." She nodded in my direction. "Only women know just how much energy and money it takes to raise these children of ours."

"Darya, I always appreciate favours. I won't let you down," Mother replied. They spoke in such hushed tones I couldn't hear half of what they were saying. The porter went to see her colleague, while Mother and I returned to our spot. On the way, I resumed my litany of hows and whys, but she immediately put a stop to my curiosity and even forbade me to mention the subject until we reached Stalingrad. Although I was hurt, I promised to be as silent as the grave, happy that it was me and not my brother to whom she had entrusted this family secret.

As we neared our bench, we saw Yosif doing 'the Georgian dance'. He always clutched himself and swung his legs about when he was desperate to pee. I stayed to keep an eye out while the boss and my brother rushed off in search of a toilet. I still couldn't get the same question out of my head: why did Mother not want to go to Central Asia with all the other refugees? I remembered father categorically stating, back in Odessa, that they would never let the Nazis advance beyond the Volga. Perhaps that was why Mother didn't want to go too far away, so that she could reach father – and our relatives – more easily. Mother returned with some food, and my brother made a makeshift table out of our suitcase and bags. In anticipation of the long-awaited meal, we sat around the appetizing packages and had barely started on our modest repast when Darya came to tell us that her colleague expected us in her office on the second floor during her lunch break. Although Mother looked the worse for wear after a sleepless night, she fixed her hair, applied powder and lipstick, and with a clean blouse, she studied herself in the small mirror with satisfaction.

The duty officer received her with a friendly manner, and invited her to sit down. First and foremost, she was interested in the jewellery. She fingered the earrings for a long time, examined them through a magnifying glass to check the make, the number of carats and the price tag. She even held them up to her ears, looking at herself in the mirror. In the end, she offered only 300 roubles rather than 375. Mother had no choice but to accept, even though she still had to pay some 100 roubles for a four-bed compartment. As for food, Mother would have to come to an arrangement herself with the conductor; if these conditions were acceptable, the duty officer would get the money and the tickets and meet her downstairs in the buffet at six o'clock, when her shift ended. Hoping for a positive outcome, Mother agreed and asked my brother and me to be her constant bodyguards for the next two hours. We gladly agreed, although we could not work out whether she was joking or being serious. Later, she explained that she was afraid to be left alone while carrying a box with expensive jewellery or a large sum of money without any insurance.

At six o'clock sharp, the duty colleague (now without her red cap) walked past, and Mother followed her to the buffet after ordering us to stay put. They sat at the staff table and were immediately served tea. In the hope of hearing something secret, Yosif and I stared at the two women calmly talking, but we didn't notice anything untoward in their exchange. When they had finished their tea, the two women parted naturally, as though they would meet again in the same place tomorrow. Not until much later, when we ourselves would have to sell our personal effects for a loaf of bread during the famine, would we realise just how dangerous it was to conduct monetary deals with a public official in wartime. For us, however, it was a true 'to be or not to be?' moment, and we couldn't fully appreciate the reasons for Mother's sadness. We spent the night in the waiting room, lying on the floor or the benches like the other refugees around us; in the morning, at ten o'clock, the woman porter took us to the train.

The conductor of the compartment carriage asked to see our tickets with some suspicion, but as soon as he read the note from the duty colleague, he helped us with our luggage and installed us in the compartment next to his own. Anna said goodbye to Darya and handed her an envelope. They both ended up in tears and embraced as they parted. The conductor arranged our luggage on the top racks. Yosif and I were assigned the middle bunks, while Mother and Roman had the lower ones. The bedding was snow white. At the end of the corridor, there was a toilet with the sign saying 'Do not use while in a station'. It made Yosif and me giggle.

"What's the matter?" asked the conductor.

I pointed at the sign. "What if you really have to go while you're in a station?"

"Well, if you really, really have to go, then go into the bushes," was the blunt reply.

Yosif was shocked. "What if the train leaves while you're in the bushes?"

"Then you run after it, and jump on," the conductor retorted.

"But it's difficult to run with your pants down," I said. The conductor burst into a loud laugh. Hearing the noise, Mother rushed out in alarm.

"What have you two done now?" The conductor stood up for us. "No harm done, Madam. You've just got two bright lads."

Mother called us back into the compartment, told us about the day's arrangements, and asked us not to bother anybody else with our questions but her, otherwise we would be spending the whole day shut up in the compartment. We gave her our Scout's word.

Our short train started, leaving the industrial city of Lugansk behind, looking dark and untidy. With its huge smoking chimneys, houses covered in soot and grimy streets, it looked nothing like our colourful Odessa. Mother persuaded us away from the window and sent us to explore the adjacent communal carriage, instructing us to stick together, to talk to no one and be back in five minutes – enough time for her to wash Roman and change his clothes. It was our first reconnaissance mission, and we would have to report our findings to the boss. A long time ago, we had played war games in the street with our friends, but it was no game now. We understood that Mother needed information, and was training our independence and initiative. Our first-class carriage seemed deserted with all the compartment doors shut. There were few people in the communal carriage, but it differed from ours in its simplicity and unpleasant smell. For some reason, the passengers eyed us with suspicion, and moved their bags away from us. Upon our return, we reported our findings, talking over each other. The conductor announced that we were approaching the junction halt and warned us that the doors would be kept shut while the carriages were linked to the main train for Stalingrad. As for meals, he said that he would give us tea but we'd have to buy food at stations during stops. The restaurant car had been closed since the start of the war because of food shortages. Once again, even in these splendid surroundings, there was yet another trial to endure. Who would run for food at every stop and be back in time? Mother with little Roman? Yosif, with his so-called 'heart condition'? No. The responsibility for errands would fall to me yet again – except that this time, it would not be just running across the street in Odessa to get bread. This time, I might have to run across several tracks carrying frequent fast trains. No thanks! There was someone older than me here. Let him do the running!

I lay on my bunk, staring out of the window. Our two carriages were being linked to the tail end of a long train. I calculated that we'd stop a long way from the actual stations, and the food stalls were usually in the middle of the platforms. You would always have to keep a hand free in case you had to grab the railing of a moving train, just as my friends and I used to do in Odessa when trying to jump onto moving trams. I was considered an expert at such tricks. If our mother had ever seen the kind of acrobatics I performed on a tram driving along the street, she would have had a heart attack. Now, however, this experience might come in useful – it could even make me the family hero and, even better, rub my older brother's nose in it.

The scarcity of food was a powerful incentive. Besides, the train proceeded at a snail's pace, frequently stopping to give priority to freight trains carrying weapons or food supplies to the front. At the first small station we stopped at, women walked alongside the carriages, selling buns with cream cheese, hard-boiled eggs, potatoes, tomatoes and various fruit. Anna leaned out of the window and called out to them, but they did not want to trudge so far down the train. The conductor, who was standing at the entrance to the carriage, suggested she give the money to one of her sons, and send him. My brother immediately ran into the compartment, but I had already caught Mum's hand and was begging her to give me the money, assuring her that I'd get back safe and sound. Grabbing a few coins from her hand, I skilfully slid down the door handrail, right past the astounded conductor.

"Look at him go!" he shouted. Our commander was shouting something after me, but I was already by the seller. "How much for the basket?" I asked, breathless. "Two roubles, son." One contained eggs and potatoes, the other, fruit. "I'll take both!" I said, handing over the money in a rush. The other hungry passengers were intent on haggling, so she pocketed the money without even counting it, while I struggled with the heavy baskets.

I wasn't sure I could manage to carry them. From the train windows, I heard cries of "Go on, boy, you can do it!"

Suddenly, I saw my brother running towards me. Mother must have booted him out of the compartment. Carrying one basket each, we reached the conductor more quickly. He cheered, then helped us onto the train.

Anna was very pale, with tears in her eyes, smiling. "Well done, boys. Only Misha, don't ever do that again. You could have been left behind," she said, squeezing my shoulder with a trembling hand. "Don't worry, Mummy, I'm a big boy now."

Once back in our compartment, she asked, "How much did all this cost?"

"Two roubles a basket." She looked puzzled. "But I only gave you three roubles in all." I hadn't counted the money, and the seller had pocketed it without checking. Yosif's attack came quickly: "On our way back to Odessa, we'll pay her the difference," he chirped, grabbing an apple from the basket. Mother stopped him, and told us to go and wash while she prepared a picnic. I was dying to ask my brother if it had been his idea to run and help me, or whether Mother had forced him. Then I suddenly remembered father warning me against becoming too arrogant. It had been after my great success playing the piano at his factory concert. That was when I first became addicted to the limelight. Astute as ever, he had taken me down a peg: "Misha, that saying of old is quite true – never love yourself in the art but the art in yourself."

Although it's sometimes nice to think of yourself as something special, above the rest, I made sure his advice was stamped on my brain, even then. I suspect father was speaking from his own experience. Although he loved music, how else would a relatively uneducated proletarian know about art?

For my seventh birthday, he bought me a splendid dark brown piano. "Go on, son," he said, "Learn to play properly. They say you have exceptional talent." Whenever he came home from work upset about something or other, Mother would whisper to me: "Go and play for father – something lyrical from your Ukrainian repertoire." So, after dinner, I would sit at the piano and softly play a few popular folk songs. Father was born and raised in Zakharievka, a village in the Odessa region, and he loved hearing the familiar tunes of his childhood. In those moments, he would usually sit on the couch and hum along as I played, gradually dozing off as he surrendered to the tiredness of his body. That was as far as his musical entertainment went. Full after our impromptu meal, lying on my bunk, I could not help but think back to peacetime. To the rhythmic sound of the train wheels, vivid faces and scenes flashed before me, as if they were only yesterday.

These reveries were, however, regularly interrupted by sudden flares and bursts of fireworks. When the sirens started, signalling the approach of Nazi planes, I woke up screaming, sat up with a start, and banged my head against the top bunk. The locomotive whistle signalled our approach to a large station. Mother smiled and patted the bump on my head, Roman laughed and Yosif teased me and threatened to tell the conductor I had broken the wooden bunk with my hard head. Naturally, I tried to punch him in the nose, but he turned away. Mother stopped us, and asked us to run to the station to buy a few bottles of lemonade or fill up the aluminium can with drinking water.

We got ready – Yosif with the can, and I with the string bag and two roubles in change in my pocket, and went for the exit. The conductor explained where we could find the water fountain and told us to get back to the train as soon as we heard the whistle. If the train had already started, we were to board the nearest carriage and find our way back to our own thereafter. Many women were crowding around the water fountain. I pushed my brother forward.

"In the Soviet Union, children don't need to queue!" I shouted, but no one paid any attention. "Yosif, don't wait for me!" I shouted over the crowd. "As soon as you've got the water, we'll meet on the train!" As usual, he tried to say something, but I was already running towards the buffet, swinging the string bag. There was no lemonade – just some dry biscuits and sweets. I asked for two roubles' worth of biscuits. The vendor weighed out quite a large paper bagful of biscuits, and pushed it into my string bag. "Give me the money," she demanded. I poured out all the coins in my pocket onto the counter.

"There should be a little more here," I lied, probably hoping that she, like the woman with the fruit basket, wouldn't check the money. Instead, this one insisted on counting every coin. I heard the train whistle. In a panic, I grabbed the purse string off the counter and dashed for the door. Someone shouted abuse after me, but the thought of the departing train carried me at lightning speed. On the platform, I could see no one at the fountain, so assumed everyone had returned to their seats. I heard my brother calling me, standing outside the carriage opposite, waving. The train suddenly moved, and the conductor pulled my brother onto the gangway. I leapt carefully over the tracks and, as I had always done, calculated the distance in relation to the accelerating train. I focused my attention on the entrance three doors away from our carriage, and ran diagonally towards it. The train was gaining speed very gradually. The doors of all the carriages were still open so as to accommodate late passengers, and the conductor standing by the third door guessed my intention. He pulled out the steps, and stood down on the top one, waiting for me. I ran a bit further along the moving train, grabbed the railing with my left hand, and prepared to push against the ground with my right foot. Swinging my left foot onto the top step, the conductor's hands grabbed me and pulled me up, along with my string bag. I was obviously not the first to board a moving train, judging by the absence of scolding, but also – to my disappointment – of any congratulation.

I waited a couple of minutes while Yosif made his way back through two carriages. "Good for you, little brother!" he cried out as soon as he saw me. It was the first time in my life that he had ever genuinely paid me a compliment. We made our way from one carriage to the next, through people and their luggage, spilling precious water, until we finally reached our compartment. Mother was not very worried, since the conductor had already told her were coming.

Waiting for me in the gangway, he asked kindly, "Hey, brave little soldier, where did you learn tricks like that?"

"On the trams in Odessa," I said proudly.

"And how old are you?"

"He's only nine," Yosif remarked dismissively.

"And a half," I added. "Why?"

"Well, I'm sure you'll amount to something," he concluded.

"But he'll always be stupid," my brother/enemy hurriedly added, leaping out of the way before I could kick him where it hurt.

"That's enough, you two!" said the conductor, placing himself between us. "They're waiting for you in your compartment. Go!"

Mother was delighted to see us back safe and sound, and thanked us for bringing the food.

After dinner, she reminded us that we'd be arriving in Stalingrad in the morning, and that we would have a very busy day formalising our evacuation, organising accommodation and so on.

"So, after dinner, we must go to bed early," she said, "to make up for the two sleepless nights we've had. We need all the energy, concentration and self-control we can muster, for this new and no doubt difficult life that awaits us in the big city, until we're reunited with father. Sleep tight."

Chapter 2

ESCAPE FROM THE NAZIS

The refugees were many on our train. On arrival in the morning, we were met on the platform by the appointed staff with Red Cross armbands. They sorted us into families with children or with old people, put us on nearby buses and took us to the various Stalingrad evacuation points. They were ancient, shabby buses that creaked and jerked over bumps on the road, prompting sighs from the adults and giggles from the children. The city looked like a military base. We passed lorries carrying soldiers, and anti-aircraft guns stood to attention in the squares; the windows of all the houses had newspaper crosses glued across them, to prevent the glass from shattering in air raids. Such sights provoked great curiosity in the children, but the adults reacted differently. Fears of an uncertain and dangerous future were ingrained on their anxious faces. Mother kept staring through the cracked window of the bus. Her instinct, which unfailingly signalled impending danger, now warned her that our prospects in Stalingrad were grim. Possibly, even fatal.

The bus stopped outside a sumptuous villa that looked like a museum, with a garden surrounded by high railings. We were lead into an enormous hall, where our documents were taken, and we were asked to store our luggage temporarily in the basement. After that, we all went up to the second floor, where everyone was placed according to available space. Our family was offered a large, bright room, where four of the existing twenty-four camp beds were still unoccupied. The official explained that this was Hall No. 3, and was reserved for unaccompanied mothers. There was a nanny permanently on hand to help with infants, a separate toilet and bathroom, a library and a medical centre on the first floor. She also said there was a post and telegraph office nearby, a tram stop across the street, hot water, working heating, and that the accommodation was free of charge.

There were two leisure courts in the gardens of the evacuation campus – one a children's playground, the other a sports field for older children. I spent practically all day playing football, volleyball, drafts and other games with my peers. Yosif was also lucky enough to be able to read library books in the garden; Mother took Roman to the playground. Everyone went to eat and sleep at the same time. While the little one was playing, our mother and her fellow residents chatted about the war, their families, and the local problems.

From the very first day, our mother – a hygiene fanatic – was taken aback by the carelessness of the administrative staff towards new arrivals. Of our group, no one was asked anything about where we had come from or how we had travelled to get here. No medical checks were carried out before living in such overcrowded accommodation. No training was given on elementary personal hygiene when living in close quarters with other families. Many children would arrive in such a dirty state at mealtimes that the server had to send them to wash before eating. There was no laundry, except for a few bowls in the communal toilet in the basement, and some washing lines in the garden. Most of the residents never changed their clothes, and stank accordingly. All the mothers worried about an epidemic, and duly complained to the management but all they were told by way of reply was that all the rooms and toilets were washed and disinfected every day. As for personal hygiene, that was the responsibility of the evacuees themselves. This answer did not satisfy Mother. She went straight to the manager and warned: "If my children catch anything, I will start legal proceedings against you personally, on the grounds of professional incompetence."

The manager glared at Mother, aware that, in this instance, she could not fob her off with an empty promise.

"Have you finished?" she asked, sternly.

"For now," Mother replied, marching out with the decisive gait she adopted in such situations. That very evening, notices were put up on the door of every room, summoning all the residents – including the children – to a meeting on the first floor after breakfast, at ten a.m. It seemed this meeting was the result of a telephone conversation between the manager and the municipal authorities. The manager obviously did not want to take on the responsibility for the refugees' personal hygiene. Mother was getting ready for her role at the meeting. Early that morning, she told us to scrub thoroughly, wear clean shirts and wipe the thick layer of dust off our shoes. Some of the other mothers also brought their children along spotlessly groomed, but by no means all. Obviously, not everyone had a change of clothes, or the means to buy one. They could not understand the reason for this meeting and were a little concerned.

The manager began the meeting by insisting on the observance of the house regulations on display by the main entrance. "The report we have received from the sanitary inspectors," she continued, "States that many residents are not complying with basic personal hygiene, which could lead to an epidemic of disease. For this reason, starting from today, I will not allow anyone into the dining room with unwashed hands or unreasonably dirty clothes. Please do not remove the soap from the communal toilet in the basement, and use your own towels. Are there any questions?"

Nobody spoke. Looks were exchanged. Anna raised her hand. "I have a question and a request. Could you please put extra washing lines in the basement?" There .

was a clapping of hands. "And another thing. Could you please ask the city council to give a small allowance to enable those single mothers in dire need to buy a change of clothes for their children? I don't mean me. That will make it easier for them to keep their children clean, and not put others at risk."

The hall fell silent while the manager conferred with the municipal official next to her. Then, surprisingly, she spoke directly to our mother. "Please urgently draw up a list of all the children in need, specifying their ages – no older than thirteen. The social department will look at your application and provide this assistance." And so it was that after the meeting, just three days after our arrival at the evacuation point, my mother was appointed leader of the community. The other women started coming to her with complaints and for advice. As far as she could, she listened to them and advised them even though she had enough on her plate already, with us three to deal with. Trouble, however, was just around the corner.

As expected, the municipality did nothing. The hygiene in the evacuation point deteriorated noticeably. Eight days after we moved in, one of the women's small children was taken ill almost at the same time. The nurse assumed that their fever and vomiting was food poisoning. Anna discovered that they had not been vaccinated against scarlet fever, measles, smallpox or other contagious childhood diseases. She gathered together the mothers of the other children to explain the potential dangers, and they went to the manager and demanded that a doctor be called immediately, as they were all sharing a room with the sick children. The manager said that the city hospitals were crammed with wounded from the front, and that all the doctors were so busy that they came out only in exceptional cases.

"This is precisely the kind of case which could lead to tragedy," protested our Bagheera. "I have asked the other mothers, and in our room there are only four teenagers apart from my two boys who have been inoculated. The other thirteen, including my youngest, have no protection whatsoever."

"You're putting our children's lives at risk," chimed the other women, "And you will be held responsible!"

The manager called the nurse, instructed her to take the sick children immediately into isolation at the medical centre, and call for the doctor straight away. The doctor promised to come the next morning, but another child was taken ill that same night. This time, an ambulance was called, and all three children were taken to hospital, where measles was diagnosed. Medical teams arrived in the morning and occupied the entire evacuation point; in an obvious panic, they disinfected every corner of the building and isolated all the occupants of our room in a purpose-built annexe with a separate entrance from the garden. All these safety measures were too little, too late, however. Children who had not been vaccinated against measles were taken ill, one after another, almost daily. They were urgently taken to hospital with their mothers. There were only four healthy children left: Yosif, myself, and two sisters who, like us, had been vaccinated. Their mother kindly looked after us while our mother had to go to the hospital twice a day to nurse Roman.

In the hospital, the situation reached catastrophic proportions. The children could not be treated because of the shortage of medicines. Priority went to the wounded, so that they would recover as soon as possible to be sent back to the front. In time of war, sick children were apparently less worthy of medical attention and trying to save them in these circumstances seemed frankly almost impossible. Unable to prevent impending death, the medics turned away in shame while mothers watched their children's lives ebb away. As these women were not allowed to spend the night at the hospital, they would rush frantically out of the evacuation point every morning, with just one hope: to spend one more day with their child. Asked how long children would survive in these circumstances, the doctor could only sigh and reply, "One week at most."

Weighing the life of a sick child against that of a wounded soldier, it makes sense to save a generation rather than an individual. If a baby survives at the expense of a soldier in wartime, the enemy has a better chance of winning. If, on the other hand, the soldier is not sacrificed for the sake of the child then, once the war is won, he is likely to produce more than one child, and thus begin a new generation. Yet every mother is understandably deaf to this life and death equation. The child conceived in her womb is not merely part of her flesh and blood but the physical and spiritual bearer of her genetic inheritance. So when Mother heard that Roman might have a week left to live, she asked the doctor during one of her visits what he would do if this were his own child, given the lack of effective medication.

"In the old days," he said in a hushed tone, "They used to treat measles with honey and chicken broth. That's all I can say." Mother thanked him and told Roman that she would travel to the far distant market the very next day to buy him a chicken, and that Yosif would be looking after him all day instead. While I played with Roman in his ward, Anna went to find out from the hospital staff where in Stalingrad she could buy honey and fresh poultry. At first they smiled, thinking she was joking, but then advised her, in chorus, to go out of town where, in one of the small villages, there may still be honey and live birds. That evening, our commander-in-chief warned Yosif that he would have to take her shift at the hospital for a day or two to take care of the little one, while she and I would go in search of medicine.

At dawn the next morning, we walked all the way to the central station and took the bus southeastwards. About an hour into the journey, Mother asked our fellow travellers where we could buy honey and chicken for a sick child. They gave her the name of a nearby village with a larger population than its surrounding hamlets. As we were getting off, the driver forewarned us that he'd be driving through on his way back in four hours' time, but would not wait. We had only three hours for our search.

The first thing we did was go into the village shop opposite the bus stop to ask where we were most likely to find the provisions we sought. The shopkeeper came out on the porch and pointed us in the direction of large farms on the edge of the village. Her eyes followed us for a long time, wondering what could possibly have brought us here, in the middle of nowhere. We had no luck in the first two houses, but were met at the third by a large dog and its miniature owner. "What do you want?" she shouted. Mother briefly recounted our plight. The woman studied her from top to toe, then me. Then she hushed the barking dog and pronounced, quite firmly, "There's no bee honey – only watermelon honey. Maybe we can find you a chicken, too. But how exactly are you, a tramp, planning to pay? Money's no good to anyone, nowadays. Have you got anything more valuable in there?" she said, pointing at Mother's handbag.

Mother took out a paper bag, and unwrapped a beautiful burgundy velvet tablecloth embroidered with gold thread. Surprised, the woman quickly stopped her, looked around, and invited us into the house. In the parlour, she spread out this rare example of fine craftsmanship on her table, checking for hidden flaws. "You didn't steal this, did you?" she sneered.

"Wedding present," replied Mother through gritted teeth. The women crossed glances like duellists, but said nothing. "All right," said the peasant. "I'll give you two jars of honey and a chicken for this. All right?"

Mother nodded, and we followed the woman into the inner courtyard. On the way, I keep pinching myself to wake myself up. I thought this must all be a dream – scenes from a play. How is that possible, I wondered? How did Mother know that the tablecloth would be worth more than the money she had such trouble obtaining? Why is she tolerating being called a thief by this woman?

There was a vegetable garden in the yard with a large tree stump in the middle. The peasant woman told us to wait while she went indoors and came out a few minutes later bearing two jars of honey, which she placed in front of my mother on an earth mound. Then, she went to the hen house. The din of squawking birds soon died down as she emerged carrying her a cackling hen upside down, by its legs. Evidently used to doing this, she picked up an axe, flung the hysterical bird over the tree stump and, with a decisive swing, chopped off its head and threw the fluttering carcass on a nearby pile of hay. Mother quickly covered my eyes with her hand, but I could still see through the gaps in her fingers how, in the throes of death, the head and body kept jerking independently from each other in different parts of the yard. I felt my flesh crawl.

"You can take it once the blood stops," said the peasant woman gruffly as she stepped into the pantry. I felt I was going to be sick. Mother dragged me to a water tap in the corner of the yard, splashed my face with cold water and, cupping her hand, made me drink a couple of sips. The woman came out with a rope and a dirty feedbag. She tied the bird's throat firmly, put it into the feedbag, and placed it next to the honey. Then she said, "Here are your goods. Now go, and God bless."

We were taken aback by such rudeness. Still, we rushed back to the bus stop. The village shop was still open. Mother went in to buy us some underwear, socks and a few other essentials while I watched out for the bus. Back home in Odessa, everyone knew my piratical whistle signal. On the way home, I asked Mother where she was going to cook the chicken, and if she thought Roman had the strength to eat it all by himself. She smiled. "The cook at the evacuation point will prepare the chicken for something special in return."

I was curious. "Money or jewels?"

"Whatever seems appropriate. It's not up to me."

"How will you pay when you have no more precious things left?"

"Time will tell," she replied, evading the question. "As for the chicken, Roman can only drink the thick broth, so the meat is for the family – you included – to eat."

I smiled to myself, anticipating the taste of chicken, which I had not had for over two months. "And what are you going to do with the second jar of honey?"

"I'm going to share it with my neighbour. Her daughter is the same age as Roman, and she's also in hospital."

"Oh, Dina," I said. "I don't understand why we have to give things away to strangers, when we had such trouble getting them ourselves."

"First of all, they are not strangers. They're our people. We live together. And, secondly, Dina's mother often looks after Roman while I have to leave the hospital to take care of us all. She helps me out like a close friend, and I want to give her something in return. And, finally, Dina and her mother are very poor, and can't afford to buy medicine. If we don't help, the little girl might die. Is that what you want?"

"In that case, we must be sure to share the chicken broth, too," I exclaimed.

"This must all be a secret," Mother replied. "If people find out where we've been today, we could get into a lot of trouble, so hold your tongue."

"I won't say a word to anyone, I promise."

We were late for dinner, but the cook allowed Mother to prepare the chicken in the storeroom. She made the broth herself after everyone had gone to bed, so that no one would bother her. Dina's mother gave us the day's news, and said the medical team had decided to transfer two sick children into a separate ward reserved for those for whom there was no hope left. The next morning, out of the thirteen sick children, only eleven remained. When the doctor came on his rounds, he prescribed Dina and Roman boiling water with honey twice a day, on an empty stomach and, for lunch, a large bowl of broth. He said that if they could maintain this diet for three days, there might be hope of recovery for them. At the evacuation point, the parents of sick children walked past one another in silence, not even looking up. Numbed, they waited for the end of their loved ones, powerless. As the week went by, every day claimed one or two victims until only Dina and Roman were left. Eleven little lives lost through lack of medicines – eleven victims sacrificed in the name of the future.

Hitler's men had slowed down but were approaching with renewed tenacity. In the evening, the horizon was once more bathed in the glow of silent explosions. We couldn't wait for Roman to be fully recovered before running away from the enemy yet again. Mother wanted to go to Saratov, but there was no direct train. We were forced to buy double-priced tickets on the black market to Kamyshina and to take a bus from there.

Parting with Dina and her mother was very emotional. Our Bagheera was secretly proud of saving the little girl's life, and how this act had brought her closer to her mother, who was on her own and who would inevitably have to be left behind. Charity begins at home, they say; survival is a rule of nature, unalterable. And so it was with a heavy heart that we embarked on yet another journey, to face yet more adventures.

The winter of 1941–42 was harsh. The bitter November cold forced us to wear half our luggage on our bodies. Mother sold the suitcase containing father's things at a crowded market in Stalingrad; she had hoped against hope for as long as she could that he would come for us, and may wish to change his uniform for civilian clothes. But at this point, even we children knew that the end of the war was far from near. With each item of father's clothing she sold, she gave a deep sigh, as though parting with him forever. Even so, she insisted that father was alive and thinking of us. "We'll all be together again, and soon."

The long train was crowded with refugees being evacuated to Kazakhstan, and we reached Kamyshina without any problems, hardly ever stopping. However, when we arrived at the bus station, there was a long queue at the closed ticket window. "Wait here," Anna ordered, with a hopeless hand gesture. Grabbing Roman, she left the hall and went to the bus park, in search of the driver of the Saratov bus. After a half hour, she returned, apologising for the delay. She told us that our bus was leaving in an hour, and that we had to eat before that. The rickety old bus was packed with local women with empty baskets after selling fruit and vegetables on the Stalingrad market.

At nightfall, we stopped to sleep in a large farm by the roadside. The driver told us that the road was closed to civilian transport in order to leave room for military vehicles. The women with baskets who came from neighbouring villages left in different directions. In the coaching inn, we were given some tasty soup, and there were straw mattresses laid out side by side on the ground for us to sleep on. The hot food and the smell of freshly baked bread warmed us up. We slept like logs, until the driver woke us up before dawn, urging us to get ready. We were about an hour and a half away from Saratov. The bus proceeded slowly in the semi-darkness, its headlamps unlit because of the blackout. At one point, the driver stopped the bus and stepped out onto the road. We saw the familiar flares on the horizon ahead of us, followed by the dull echo of explosions. The horizon was aglow with red from the fires. The passengers stood still, rooted to the spot in fear, afraid to break the silence. "Horses!" said the driver, as though giving the order to himself. As we drew closer to the city, we heard the growing sound of ambulances and fire engine sirens.

The driver said that the Nazis had been bombing the city for four nights, and that there were many dead and injured in the streets. He added that he would regrettably not be able to drive us all the way, but would do his best to take us as far as the central bus station, where they would help us to continue on our journey. Yosif's eyes and mine were popping out of their sockets. Thanks for nothing, I thought – dumping us like that! Mother tried to calm us down, promising that we would not be staying in Saratov long. The other passengers were talking anxiously to one another and, in panic, all fired questions at the driver at the same time. He calmed the general hysteria with a brusque honk of the horn: "I need total silence here, so I can concentrate on getting you to the city centre."

At the entrance to the city, the duty patrol told the driver the best way to get to the central bus station. For the first time, we saw from up close firemen bravely trying to extinguish fires, nurses carrying the injured into ambulances, soldiers from an engineering regiment digging in the ruins of a house in the hope of saving people trapped in underground shelters. No wonder elderly policemen kept stopping our bus, demanding to know how the driver had got there and what these poor refugees were doing in a burning city. The passengers, in total shock, resigned themselves to their fate. But not our Bagheera. We could see, deep in her eyes, that she was hatching a new plan of escape.

At the bus station, posters announced that three days earlier, on 7th November, all local and inter-city bus services in the Volga region would be suspended, and the buses handed over to the garrison for transporting the wounded. Passenger trains and city trams would continue as normal, however. Refugees were requested to go to the municipality for help regarding their evacuation inland, and all the passengers rushed to the tram stop – except our own commander-in-chief. She took us to the toilet and made us wash and comb our hair before going to the station buffet. After tea and a snack, she went with Roman to sort things out, leaving my brother and me with the boring task of looking after the luggage. When Mother finally returned, Roman ran towards me, brandishing a new toy – a torch, which an unknown female driver had given him in the bus yard. Mother had spent a long time discussing with her the possibility of travelling north, alongside the Volga, where there was no rail line and now, not even a bus service. Both women commiserated with each other about the hardships of life without a husband, and then she suggested to Mother the only available method of transport to the city of Marx, to which lorries returned every evening with empty containers to the food canning factory, after delivering to the military units.

Marx was an industrial town in the north of the autonomous German district. The German immigrants had recently been exiled to Siberia, thereby vacating a lot of living space for refugees. Even as recently as two days earlier, regular buses brought refugees to Marx before being requisitioned. Now, unfortunately, that option was no longer available to us. Still, we were optimistic. It was not the first time we had encountered an obstacle but, under the guide of our c-in-c, we knew we'd be safe.

"March ahead, Cossacks!" she commanded and so, hoisting our rucksacks onto our backs, we walked to the tram stop. My troubled mind was full of questions. Still, Mother must have good reason for not disclosing her plans. She must have noticed our long faces and puzzled expressions but, like the military leader I half-imagined her to be, she decided to ignore them and teach us instead to be loyal soldiers who obey authority without question. Like all children, we had blind faith in our mother, and would have happily followed her to the ends of the earth. If we sometimes complained and whinged, it was because we were genuinely exhausted by the constant travelling, and missed our father, friends and normal lives.

The tram arrived, empty and without a conductor. Anna asked the driver how many stops it was to the petrol station. "The second stop after the city council," he said in a weary, wheezing voice. "If the German machine guns or bombs start," he added, "throw yourselves down on your sandbags and cover your heads with your hands." It was only then that we noticed that the side windows of the tram had been replaced with plywood, while the front and back window had no panes at all.

"What about the fares?"

"No fares," came the curt reply, as he noisily started the engine. There were hardly any passengers at the stop – a few boys would occasionally leap onto the tram, and chase after each other. They reminded me of my own escapades on the trams in Odessa. Roman was asleep on Mother's lap, Yosif was taking in the town through the back window while I kept replaying in my memory pleasant episodes of life during peace time.

Suddenly, my reverie was interrupted by the loud wail of sirens. The driver braked and yelled, "Get down!" before throwing himself on the floor by his seat. Mother covered Roman with her arms and gathered us close together on the floor, dirty and wet from the snow, with our rucksacks lying on top of us for protection. That's all we need, I thought, just as a deafening explosion happened nearby, its powerful shockwave momentarily throwing our tram a few millimetres in the air but failing to overturn it. Roman started crying, the driver moaned, and my brother and I could not speak. Our commander tried to ask us something, shaking us by the shoulders, but we were stunned and unable to utter a word.

The explosions were endless. The roof and walls of the tram were bombarded with shards of glass, lumps of brick and other debris. Passers-by caught up in the raid ran into our tram for shelter, many already bleeding from their injuries. Every minute of the bombardment felt like an eternity.

When the sirens sounded the all clear, the city filled with the wails of fire engines and ambulances. Accustomed to these attacks, the city's residents always carried first aid kits. They bandaged one another's wounds, picked up the wounded in sight, and calmed down those in shock, as though they had been doing it all their lives. The driver announced that the tram would not be going any further since it had become a medical emergency destination for the ambulance service. Mother comforted Roman, who was crying, got my brother and me ready to leave, wiped our faces with her handkerchief, perfunctorily dusted off the front of our clothes, checked that our luggage was still there and led us out of the ill-fated tram into the street.

She told us not to look around at the victims of the raid, and stick together. My brother and I nodded, still dumbstruck. The driver told Anna the quickest way to the petrol station she wanted to reach, and advised her not to walk too close to bomb-damaged buildings.

Just as it had been on the morning after the air raid, the city was filled with the blood-curdling wails of ambulances and fire engines. Having witnessed the results of the damage after being caught up in the Nazi bombing, the buildings were still miraculously in one piece. Moreover, something strange was happening to us now, after the raid. As we walked slowly down the streets of the devastated city centre, past smoking buildings, stepping over the bloody footsteps of the wounded and the dead, we felt no fear or nausea. Bizarrely, it was as though everything was as it should be. Mother kept telling us not to look in order to protect our emotions, unaware that her boys had been anaesthetised from all feelings of horror or disgust.

After walking for half an hour, we reached the main square. For some reason, the Nazis had not bombed the old municipal building itself, although many of the surrounding houses had been destroyed; perhaps, in anticipation of an easy victory, they deliberately preserved such historic sites in order to turn them into their own headquarters when the time came. There was a canteen on the other side of the square. Mother decided to stop for a rest, since Roman kept whimpering that he couldn't walk any more, and my older brother had sulked the whole way, either as a reaction to all the dramatic events or simply because he was tired and hungry. There was no food in the canteen, apart from rice soup and cold macaroni, which we ate ravenously, washed down by murky water. As the waitress was clearing our table, Mother asked her in hushed tones whether she knew anywhere one could buy vodka. The waitress reacted in disbelief, as though she had been asked for a plate of caviar.

"We're going to visit my uncle, outside town," Mother explained. "And he asked me to bring a couple of bottles. I'll make it worth your while. Please, help us."

The change in the waitress was dramatic. "Well, if it's for your 'uncle', that's different. I'll ask cook – he knows everybody."

When she walked away, Yosif and I both stared questioningly at Mother, wanting to know. She simply smiled and whispered: "Just eat your macaroni, you two, and don't meddle in adult business. It's nothing to do with you." Rebuffed, we returned our attention to our plates, knowing full well that argument was futile whenever the boss took that tone.

Roman was still eating his soup when the waitress unexpectedly placed half a glass of milk before him.

"Compliments of the chef," she said. Wiping the table with a cloth, without looking at Anna, she whispered, "There's only homemade vodka. Twenty roubles for two bottles." Mother nodded her acceptance and then thanked her in a loud voice for the milk.

"When you're ready to go, I'll see you out," said the waitress before walking away again.

After we finished eating, Mother took Roman to the ladies' toilet, while Yosif and I went to the gents'. On the way, she told Yosif to transfer his books from his rucksack to mine. "Twenty roubles!" he protested, "That's a fortune!"

I replied with father's maxim: "Our lives are worth more." Putting his books into my rucksack, Yosif wondered why.

"To make room for the package the waitress is going to give us," I replied, as if it were obvious. They were waiting for us as we came out of the toilet. Mother took Yosif's rucksack, and gave him hers. He was about to say something, but one look from Bagheera stopped his tongue. The waitress came out with us into the canteen entrance hall and exchanged the package she held for the agreed sum and gave directions to the petrol station. As we left, Mother slipped the package into Yosif's rucksack, put it on her shoulders and helped him to put on hers which, although larger, was also lighter. Only then did she explain to us that cash was not always the best bargaining tool for unofficial deals. As it turned out, she eventually had to pay both bottles of vodka for our next trip north.

"I'm telling you this in confidence," she said, "It's a secret, so don't let on."

It didn't take us long to walk two tram stops. There was a large garage for vehicle repairs at the petrol station. Mother found the supervisor and mentioned the name of the woman driver from the central bus depot. He introduced himself as Ivan Petrovitch, and started asking us who we were, where we were from and how he could help us. Mother showed him her documents, and asked him to recommend a responsible lorry driver who would be making the unloaded return trip to the town of Marx that evening, after his delivery.

"I'll make it worth your while," she promised. Upon this, the garage supervisor looked at us attentively, his eyes lingering on Roman. "Many refugees have been using this route lately, but they're adults who can bear the discomfort of travelling in an open truck. Winter's coming, all night on the road, and here's a mother with little ones. Anything could happen." He seemed to be talking to himself. "Madam, you're taking a big risk with your family. You must assume all responsibility," he said.

"It's still better than what we went through twice right here in your city today," Anna protested, "And tomorrow may be even worse. We can't just stay here and wait to be killed when there's even a small chance of saving ourselves. Please help us, Ivan Petrovitch."

"All right, all right," he said, trying to pacify the woman, who was clearly upset. "I don't want anything from you, Anna. I'll do everything I can to help your family, in my capacity as a Council Deputy, but I'll not be held responsible for your journey. You need to give me a disclaimer, that you're making this journey and have made an agreement with the driver entirely on your own account, and that you take full responsibility for yourself and your children."

He handed Mother a sheet of paper and a pen. Once she had signed the document, Ivan Petrovitch told us to wait while he went into the garage. When he returned, he told us that there were two vehicles bound for Marx that night, and one of the drivers was prepared to take us, so long as we were dressed for winter, including hats and gloves. Aghast, Mother looked at her watch. "But we've only got half an hour before the shops close," she said weakly.

"We've got time," he said. "I'll give you a lift in the breakdown van. Leave your luggage here in my office, and don't forget to take money with you."

We rushed to the shops, piled on top of one another in the commodious cab. While Ivan Petrovitch waited for us in the van, we ran up and down the shop floors, buying winter clothes. Even young Roman tried to keep up, shouting, "Wait for me! Wait!"

Without taking time to choose, Mother grabbed bootees, leg warmers, jackets, jumpers and other warm clothing, only stopping long enough to make sure they were the right size for every child. Seeing us return laden with heaps of clothing, the garage supervisor burst out laughing. He loaded our shopping into the van, and then drove us to the nearest grocery. The three of us stayed in the van while Ivan Petrovitch went shopping with Mother. He explained that if he accompanied her, she would be able to buy produce that was not normally on general sale, such as cheese, salami, apples and other wartime 'delicacies'. When we caught sight of foods we had not eaten for four months, we could not stop our eyes from lighting up and our mouths from drooling, but our commander was firm: "Not now. We'll have our feast before leaving."

Fedya, the lorry driver, was waiting for us at the garage. He wore the uniform of a military supply officer. The supervisor introduced him to Anna in his office, then went to the garage. While we unpacked our shopping and tried on our new clothes, Mother spoke with Fedya to discuss essentials such as the weather conditions, the route, the safety measures and so on. She showed him the package of bottles and told him he would have one as soon as we were all loaded on the truck, and the second once we had arrived in Marx. Unshaven and in a dirty uniform, our driver didn't look too respectable but we had to make do with what we could get. Fedya outlined the plan for the journey. Mother and Roman would ride in the cab, while we two would travel in the bed of the lorry inside the empty plywood tinned food crates, under a thick tarpaulin. We were only allowed to travel lying down with our rucksacks under our heads or sitting down; on no account was standing up or even kneeling permitted. Ivan Petrovitch came in and suggested he and Fedya give us their own sheepskin army jackets to keep us warm, on condition that Fedya returned Ivan's when he was next back in Stalingrad. Mother instructed us to put everything back into our rucksacks and clear up, apologising to Ivan Petrovitch for all the mess and the trouble. He smiled, and said in Ukrainian, "That's all right. I love trouble."

The garage and filling station were open twenty-four hours a day. We took our newly packed rucksacks and bags into the entrance hall, where the workers normally had tea by a large samovar, and waited impatiently for Mother to prepare our feast. Ivan Petrovitch spent a long time talking to Fedya in his office, then came to tell us that they had agreed that should anything unforeseen happen, Fedya would transfer us into the lorry driven by his colleague Vassily, who would then get the second bottle of vodka in his stead. Wishing us luck, the supervisor said goodbye to us and gave Fedya his soft sheepskin jacket. The driver said he would be back for us at eight o'clock, and that we should be ready to go then. Mother made us wrap up as though we were travelling to the North Pole. As usual, my brother started making a fuss, but Mother would have none of it.

"If you don't do as I say, we'll leave you behind."

"What do you mean, leave me behind? Where am I going to go?"

"You'll stay here in the garage, and work for Ivan Petrovitch as an apprentice," she said.

"Great! Good riddance!" I cheered (having taken the precaution of stepping aside first).

Roman giggled, and promptly received a clip on the forehead from Yosif for his pains. Mother instantly slapped his hand. "I'm warning you, don't you ever touch the child again, or you'll be sorry."

Big brother walked away, sulking as usual. Roman, feeling sorry for him, followed and offered his little torch to play with. Anna checked our rucksacks even more carefully than usual, and repacked our luggage with the new purchases. Her maternal instinct constantly led her to anticipate the worst for the impending journey. Remembering the other times we were helped by strangers, I asked if she had remembered to thank Ivan Petrovitch.

"As I've already explained," she answered with a knowing smile, "Not everyone can be bought with money. While you were trying on your new clothes, I slipped a small keepsake into his desk drawer – a little jewellery box with a silver tie clip and matching cufflinks."

"But those are father's!" I protested.

"Before we left, father told me expressly never to spare anything if it helps to keep us safe. Jewellery comes and goes – but we only have one life."

Chapter 3

A DANGEROUS ADVENTURE

When the two lorries came for us at eight o'clock that evening, we were already at the filling station, ready for battle. After refuelling, the drivers loaded our luggage into the bed of the lorry, together with Yosif and me. Fedya arranged the deepest crates near the back window of the cabin so that we would be within sight of our mother. She and Roman took their places on the seat next to Fedya. We knocked on the window and they turned around, communicating in mime and gestures. We had no trouble understanding, and enjoyed pulling faces at one another. Both drivers had given us their sheepskin jackets as makeshift sleeping bags, and Roman and Mother had Ivan Petrovitch's large sheepskin.

The military patrol at the exit from Saratov asked Anna our destination, and why we were travelling at night. She explained that we travelling to Marx to join our relatives for the period of evacuation, and that since bus services had been suspended, we had to make do with whatever transport was available. She hoped that they would understand.

"How much did you pay the driver for this trip?" asked the senior officer.

"I didn't pay him anything," Mother replied without hesitation. "The station supervisor, Ivan Petrovitch, who is also a Deputy at the City Council, simply helped out the wife and three children of a soldier at the front. Is that so strange?"

The officer said nothing but gave us the nod to proceed. Throughout the exchange, Fedya sat rigidly, as though on an electric chair. Only when the barrier was lowered behind us did he sigh with relief. We rushed along the Central Volga highway until midnight, with no problems. Because of the state of emergency in the Stalingrad area, snowdrifts were regularly cleared from the roads. When we stopped to refuel, everyone disembarked to relieve themselves and restock on drinking water. The attendants warned our driver that a blizzard was forecast from the north. We had four hours to go before reaching our destination and drove as fast as we could, trying to get at least as far as the inn at the halfway point of our journey. Mother took the precaution of wrapping warm scarves around our heads, making sure we were swaddled like babies in the sheepskin jackets, and told us to keep still until our next stop, lest we turn into icicles. She put Roman on her lap and wrapped them both in the supervisor's sheepskin jacket.

We reached the inn in reasonably good shape. On the way in, Roman whimpered, cross at being awoken, and even my brother and I dragged our feet, half asleep. Inside, the landlady was blowing on the coals of the samovar in the heated parlour, and warmly invited us to enjoy homemade gingerbread and fragrant tea. We were only too happy to disentangle ourselves from the bounds of our voluminous clothing and climb up beside the stove while Mother got to know the landlady, exchanging notes about their respective families. The last thing we heard before falling asleep was the wall clock striking midnight.

After a lengthy tea break by the samovar with the women, the drivers decided to resume the journey in order to reach Marx by dawn. They wanted to avoid being seen carrying any passengers at all, let alone children. While they started the engines, Mother once again hastily wrapped us in the friendly embrace of the old clothing. The landlady said the blizzard had eased off, but the frost was now even more severe. She offered some homemade lard to rub on our hands and faces. Mother overruled our vain protests. As soon as we stepped outside, we were hit by the icy cold. Vassily packed us snugly in the sheepskin jacket into the crate, and forbade us to fall asleep, while Fedya helped Mother and Roman.

After driving along the snowy road for about an hour, our lorry suddenly lurched sideways. Behind us, Vassily sounded his horn. We had to stop. The drivers examined the left rear wheel. It turned out that one of the inner bolts had fallen out. While Fedya checked that all the other nuts were tight, Vassily looked for a replacement bolt in his stock of spares, but couldn't find anything suitable. They walked back along the road, shining torches in an attempt to find the lost bolt, but with five or six centimetres of fresh snow on the ground, it was pointless.

We complained that our feet were freezing. Mother made sure that Roman, asleep on the seat, was wrapped up, and then helped us out of the lorry bed. The three of us started running up and down the road, counting out thirty paces each way. She kept telling us to breathe only through our noses, and reminded us that we had handkerchiefs in our left pockets. As ever, she was remarkably perceptive and well organised. Motherhood, for her, had nothing to do with romantic illusions or soppy sentimentality. It was purely a matter of dedication and elbow grease. Raising and educating three very different and wilful sons on one's own was no picnic. Though out of breath, she kept pace with us, racing up and down in the knowledge that her children's lives depended on it.

Back in Odessa before the war, we lived next door to a woman called Sasha, who would stand in for Mother when she went shopping or out with father in the evenings. From an early age, she fed us, wiped our noses and bottoms, and read us adventures from the Bible as bedtime stories. Once when I was walking with her in the neighbourhood park, we saw Soviet atheists remove the gilded bells and cross from the white church with three domes. It was a scary sight for a five-year-old. When I asked Sasha why they were doing it, she burst into tears and fell to her knees. I remember how devastated she was, bowing and crossing herself. I stood next to her, frightened, unable to comprehend what was wrong with her. A few passers-by surrounded us, forming a shield against prying eyes.

Running with us to prevent us from freezing, Anna looked as though she was praying, her hands folded over her chest. We had all been brought up as non-believers until that winter of 1941, when a miracle happened. Yosif saw it first: "Look, Mummy, look! Something's coming!"

It was a military convoy bound for Stalingrad. It turned out that the soldiers had noticed us from afar, and had come back to check what we were doing stopped in the middle of the road. They comforted Anna, who was crying. Unaware of the danger we had faced, we began chatting to the soldiers. One of them threw an overcoat over Mother's shoulders while another gave her water from a flask. She kept thanking them and calling them her kind saviours.

Our drivers returned from their fruitless search. The senior officer heard them out, and ordered one of his drivers to bring the part required. He took our unfortunate drivers aside and said something very sternly with frequent nods in our direction. While the drivers replaced the missing bolt, the officer told Mother whom to contact at the evacuation centre in Marx. He confirmed the wisdom of settling in the German district of the Volga region as a good place to await the end of hostilities. The soldiers put us back into the bed of the newly repaired lorry, wrapped us up, then jumped off with easy agility. They joined the officer in saluting us, and wishing us a good journey.

Tired after all the running about and much warmer, Yosif and I dozed for the remainder of the journey. Mother, on the other hand, kept replaying the incident in her mind. Women have a keener sense of self-preservation than men, and she couldn't rest until her doubts were assuaged. Why didn't Fedya check all the nuts and bolts before setting off? How come neither driver carried spare parts? Why did they both have to go looking for the lost bolt, without even leaving one engine running to keep the children warm? How could they be away for so long, leaving us like that without a thought for the consequences? What did the officer say to Fedya when he took him aside? Could Soviet young people possibly be prepared to harm children for the sake of gain? Such questions, and many others, remained unanswered in her mind.

We eventually unloaded by the municipal building in Marx city centre, and Mother handed Fedya the second bottle of vodka with less than effusive thanks. Without even apologising for his negligence, he hurried off as though nothing had happened. Our Bagheera stared after him for a long time, as though trying to find the answers to her niggling questions. The doors to the building were still shut, but the duty policeman was glad to tell us when they would open. He suggested that we leave our bulky luggage in behind the pillar of the portico and wait in the tearoom across the street, which would be warmer and more comfortable than standing outside. Without even waiting for Mother's permission, Yosif and I sprinted towards the prospective meal. We can't have looked very presentable, since the woman at the counter immediately adopted a defensive pose, but relaxed when she saw Mother approach with Roman. She turned out to be a friendly woman, and offered a fresh towel when she heard that we refugees had just arrived and were waiting for the municipal offices to open. As usual, Mother's priority was to take us to the toilet.

When we returned to the table, it was a delightful surprise to find four plates of steaming porridge, four glasses of kvass and a beaming hostess. We cheered. We gobbled the porridge, suspending the rules of etiquette that normally prevailed in our family until, sated, we leaned back against our chairs. Only then did we notice how tired Mother looked. The neat hairstyle and face powder could not hide the dark rings of sleepless nights under her eyes. She looked older than when we were back in Odessa. Yosif could not help asking, "Mummy, will we ever stop moving from one place to another?"

I too stared into her eyes, echoing my brother's query. Roman's spoon seemed to pause in his mouth, as though awaiting an explosive response, even though all was quiet. At first Mother frowned, then gave a deep sigh.

"My darling boys, I understand your feelings entirely, and don't blame you for them," she said. "In fact, I'm surprised you didn't ask sooner. Many other children would have started whining and throwing tantrums by now. You've had to endure so many journeys – such strenuous journeys too, at your age – without your father's help, without any experience of travelling, and with a baby brother in tow. You've been patient throughout it all – impressively so. I want you to know that as your mother, I'm immensely proud of you and have a great deal of respect for your forbearance. You do credit to your father. I'm sure I don't have to explain why we keep having to move. At the start of the war, the Soviet people blindly trusted the words of our great leader when he said that the Nazis would never reach the Volga. You also know that after our victory, father will come and find us and we'll all go and live in either in Siberia or in Central Asia. We've already talked about this many times. It's true that we were wrong to leave Odessa quite so soon. But how could anyone know that the war, which was supposed to be over in four weeks, would still be going on after four months? Tell me, what would you have done in my shoes? Would you have disobeyed your father? Would you have given yourselves up to be massacred by the enemy? When there's a war on, things sometimes turn out differently from the way you planned them. If you don't follow the laws of survival, you die. It's a rule of nature. Even animals know that. In answer to your question as to how much longer are we going to move from place to another, the answer is that I simply don't know. Adults need very little – just a job and a roof over their head. But children need much better living conditions, schooling and so on. So we'll keep moving until we find what we need." Then she fell silent.

"Seek and ye shall find," I said, in the words of a popular song. Yosif gave me a dirty look, and pulled a disgusted expression from his range of grimaces. To prevent another fight, Mother told us to stop quarrelling because that was unhelpful. We duly lowered our heads.

They were already expecting us at the municipal offices, as the policeman had told them of our arrival. After they had checked our documents, they registered us to live in the village of Hussinbach, in the north-east of the region. They gave Mother a letter of introduction to the chairman of the village council and provided a minibus to get us there. Without further ado, the manager of the social department gave Anna, as the wife of a serving soldier with three children, the financial assistance to which we were entitled. In the circumstances, the amount covered one or two weeks of modest living expenses per month. Mother would therefore have to find work at least part-time. Given that the accommodation was free of charge, including electricity, water and heating, the allowance was more than acceptable in wartime.

Comfortably installed in the eight-seater minibus, we began the two-hour journey hoping that this would be our last move. We dreamed of a peaceful schoolboy life with new friends, spending our free time ice-skating or skiing, and things like going to town to buy a Christmas tree. Outside, the road had been swept, and there were tall snow banks on each side. Behind them stretched endless forest, part green and part white – the rugged beauty of winter. We had never seen anything like this in Odessa, so we stared in amazement.

First, we headed east, then north for the second part of our journey. This road, to Hussinbach, had not been cleared of snow. Like us, Mother was admiring the beautiful winter landscape when her face was suddenly filled with horror at the sight of something outside the window. On both sides of the road, blanketed in snow, lay the bodies of farm animals that had frozen to death where they had fallen, in grotesque poses. Yosif and I were hysterical: "Mummy, are we going to a graveyard?"

Frightened by the sudden screams, the driver stopped the bus. "What's the matter with you?" he thundered. "Never seen dead cattle before?"

Mother gave him her Bagheera look. "Instead of shouting at my children, why don't you explain the reason for this horror?"

The driver lowered his tone in contrition. He explained that the last of the German immigrants from the 1930s had vacated the surrounding area in a rush only the week before. Every family had been allowed just one ox cart to transport the entire household, including old people, children and domestic animals. The adults and other cattle had to make their way on foot as far as

Urbach train station, from where they were taken by freight train to Buryat, in Mongolia. Unlike people, the animals could not withstand the strain, and died along the way.

"That's all I know," concluded the driver.

At Hussinbach village council, we were received by the elderly chairman, Victor Nikolayevitch. He studied our papers, signed a receipt for the consignment of the refugees, and dismissed the driver. His secretary, Nastya, came in and smiled: "Welcome to our autonomous district!"

"Do you mean the 'German' district?" asked Yosif, trying to be clever. Nastya busied herself by the samovar in the corner of the room, and pretended not to hear.

"It used to be German," snapped the chairman. He changed the subject, and asked the refugee, "So what brings you out into the sticks so far from the city, my dear?"

"The hope that we won't be pursued by Nazi aircraft," replied Mother without hesitation. "My children are exhausted after four months of moving from pillar to post, constantly followed by the war. We hope we can be safe here for the winter. Then, after our victory, their father will come for us and take us home," she added.

Nastya busied herself with clinking mugs by the samovar and announced that tea was ready, along with honey and gingerbread. Yosif and I were already distracted by the library next door, and weren't bothered about any tea, but the prospect of honey brought us promptly to the samovar table. We were surprised to find before us a bowl of hot *piroshky*, covered with a tea towel, from which escaped the appetising smell of cabbage and potatoes. We gorged ourselves on this food we had not eaten for so long with such enthusiasm that Roman almost choked – Mother had to tap him on the back to dislodge the unfortunate piece of pie from his throat.

After the generous tea and honey, we three boys returned to the library while our mother stayed with Victor Nikolayevitch and Nastya to sort out accommodation, schooling, the possibility of a part-time job and so on. Nastya told the chairman that the heating had already been turned on in our new home, but that we would have to pick up food on our way there, and fresh water from the well.

"Follow me, Musketeers!" ordered our commander. That made Victor Nikolayevitch and Nastya laugh. "You truly are a brave woman, Anna," they said. "I don't know how you manage them so well."

"I have a six-year-old boy, and he's got me wrapped up around his little finger," Nastya confessed.

"I'm a qualified teacher," Mother replied. "It helps to have experience in dealing with children."

Victor Nikolayevitch and his secretary exchanged glances and said there was a good chance our mother would get a job. Now that all the German schoolchildren had gone, there was hardly anyone left in the classrooms, so the teachers had relocated to the cities. He said that if Anna were interested, he would ask the headmistress of the village school if they could start a mixed class with a basic curriculum for seven to ten-year-olds in order to free their parents to work at the local collective cattle-breeding farm. She would only have to work four hours a day, from eight to twelve, with the rest of the day free to take care of her own family. Mother hesitated and admitted that she had not taught for years, and would have to refresh her memory in history, geography, literature and other subjects. She said she could possibly manage it if the headmistress would help her with the necessary materials, but would only do it for six months – until the end of the academic year. The chairman nodded in approval.

The house we were allocated turned out to be huge, with four rooms, a kitchen, a parlour but no shower or toilet – but that was usual in a 1940s village. It had a spacious garden surrounded by a tall fence, with two largish barns for farm animals and household tools, and also produce for the residents. In the middle of the garden there was a well for drinking water and, in the corners, a supply of firewood and hay, as well as agricultural and farming equipment. There were various things scattered around the place, as proof of the previous owners' hasty departure, and their agony at having to leave their home and their belongings.

They had left a lot of crockery and kitchen utensils behind in the house, but no blankets or bedding, towels, curtains or other soft furnishings. Nastya appreciated Mother's predicament and promised, by the following day, to buy in the village shop or get from the other inhabitants all the ingredients of a normal life for children who had been deprived of home comforts for the past four months. She helped Mother draw up a list of all that was missing in the house, and then gave her the keys to the gates, doors and windows. Before leaving, Nastya lit two paraffin lamps and left some matches. She also showed us the toilet in the garden, and the indoor washbasins in the pantry. As soon as she had left, we all just flopped on the unmade beds and couches without even undressing. Mother bolted all the doors, and joined us.

The next morning, on our way to the village council office, we passed many deserted houses with their blinds shut. Solid fences stood high on both sides of the street. The former residents obviously either preferred to keep themselves to themselves or were worried about being burgled. The previous evening, when we had driven in the minibus past the scattered military barracks, the driver said that they had all been prison camps before the war. Most of the inmates had gone to the front, while the most dangerous had been sent to the Urals. Some had managed to escape from the train and were undoubtedly still hiding in the woods that he pointed out.

At the village shop, we met the headmistress, Vera Yakovlevna, who made a good impression on us. She asked no questions, but took Mother into a different room to discuss the chairman's suggestion. After eight hours of uninterrupted sleep, we were all feeling much stronger, and Mother even had a chance to clean herself up so that she looked like a proper teacher. The three of us rushed to the now familiar library, back to the magazines we had not finished reading the day before. Nastya gave us gingerbread and honey again and asked us to be quiet while she went to buy all the things we needed for our comfort. We couldn't believe that we had finally found a stable home.

Vera Yakovlevna and Anna discussed the school curriculum for a mixed group of young children. The school had not reopened in September, since most children had left. Only about thirty of last year's pupils remained, who were due to start in the second to fourth grades. It was agreed that they would be put in a class apart, according to their level, and taught in parallel.

Mother and Vera Yakovlevna became great friends. Vera was often invited to eat borscht with us, and they would sit and talk about the war, politics, economics and especially the nation's cultural education. When Mother asked why no one cleared the dead animals from the side of the road near the village, the headmistress explained that they could not be buried while the ground was frozen, and they were not allowed to burn them because of the proximity of military barracks, in case the animals' former owners may have poisoned or booby-trapped the beasts out of spite. There was no option but wait for the ice to thaw, when these stark reminders of human misery could be decently interred.

Nineteen forty-two was the hardest year of the war. One by one, our cities fell into enemy hands. The Soviet forces fought like lions but were unevenly matched. Yosif listened to the radio in the evenings and spouted platitudes on strategy.

"It's just like a game of chess," he said. "What our army needs to do is gather strength, and then just bash Hitler over the head." Mother would smile indulgently.

"That's easy to say, son, but to gather your strength, you have to have some in the first place, or generate it somehow. And that takes time, which is what we don't have right now. That's why we have to retreat, to gain time, disperse the enemy forces, distance the enemy from their physical base and, once their army is scattered – destroy them."

Yosif and I applauded. "Mummy, you talk like an army commander." She laughed. "It's not my plan," she said. "That's how Marshal Kutuzov dealt with Napoleon's army."

In April 1942, Mother finally received a reply from the Centre for Missing Relatives, saying that father's name was not on the list of the dead in action. On one hand, this was good news, but on the other, it meant that his whereabouts were still unknown. He could be a prisoner, or lying wounded in one of the military hospitals at the rear of the front, or missing. In any case, Mother could not stop worrying. She kept writing to various centres, without result. It was the uncertainty rather than an actual tragedy that tormented her most. My brother and

I suffered deeply but did not know how to help her. The sword of Damocles hung over our home.

The enemy, having circumvented Moscow, was slowly approaching the Volga. The front line was still far away, but that didn't prevent enemy planes from raiding distant towns in an attempt to destroy our military bases and create civilian panic. People began evacuating the Volga region in large numbers, going to the Urals or the north. At the end of the academic year, our family commander-in-chief decided to evacuate us to Kuybyshev. She told us not to breathe a word to anyone about our plans, but to concentrate solely on our forthcoming exams. At the beginning of June, she and the headmistress jointly made preparations to bring the school year to a positive conclusion. The assistants were preparing an end of term concert with the pupils on the square, and I organised a cheerful tin orchestra for the occasion.

Mother worked out that the best way to Kuybyshev was to travel up the Volga on a barge. Barges were always full on their way down to Stalingrad, but empty on their way back to Kuybyshev. The journey took three days. Barges travelled only by night, and in total darkness. Thanks to the village council library, we already fancied ourselves as pirates, partisans and hunters. We made knives, bows and arrows from wood, and Red Indian headdresses out of chicken feathers. Mother smiled indulgently. "Children, don't anticipate events. Perhaps, instead of going to Kuybyshev by barge, we'll go by flying carpet."

Roman was of course the most excited of all, galloping around the garden on a stick with a horse's mask, cracking his whip. The exams were pretty uneventful, with one subject a day. We started rehearsing on the Friday morning. The local accordionist accompanied all the acts – the songs, the dances, and the acrobatics. The percussion orchestra rehearsed last, once all the other participants went for a break before the concert. The other boys and I didn't want to divulge our eccentric act too early. It included a duel between long-handled ladles and large saucepan lids instead of swords and shields, and beating out rhythms with a rolling pin on a bucket on our heads, and so on. The whole village attended the open-air concert on the square by the council building, where travelling artists usually performed. I played the harmonica and wooden spoons; Yosif played the paper and comb. Our performance was a roaring success.

At the end of the concert, the chairman, the headmistress and Kudryavtsev (the manager of the cooperative farm) thanked Mother for her sterling work at the school and invited her to stay another academic year. Anna apologised and declined on the grounds that we were moving to Kuybyshev, where our relatives awaited us. Victor Nikolayevitch and Nastya declared that the school doors would always remain open for her, should she ever decide to return. When Kudryavtsev asked if he could help, Anna asked him to drive us to the city's wharf by car, which he agreed to with a smile at her practicality.

"When were you thinking of going?"

"Tomorrow, Saturday – or Sunday."

"What's the rush?"

"I'm worried you might change your mind."

"Very well," said Kudryavtsev. "That's what you call grabbing the bull by the horns. My daughter-in-law, Nastya, will come and pick you up on Sunday morning at nine. She's told me a lot about you."

Mother gave Nastya a hug, which made everybody laugh. We spent the whole of Saturday packing our poor belongings and saying goodbye to friends and neighbours. In the evening, the headmistress came with three members of the parents' committee. To Anna's surprise, she gave her not only her last pay packet, but also a prize from the chairman: "You will find this very useful now," Nastya remarked.

Unable to put her feelings into words, Mother invited everyone to sit around the table. When she returned from the kitchen with a bowl of homemade *piroshky*, there was already on the table a can of kvass, a bottle of homemade vodka, gherkins, smoked herring, and a pot of hot jacket potatoes. Everyone laughed at the sight of my mother's astounded look.

"Vera Yakovlevna, what's all this?" Anna asked in a reproachful tone.

"It's to wish you a good trip, Anna dear. May God bring you and your Musketeers every success!"

The women all clinked glasses and sipped homemade vodka with wedges of crusty bread. Noticing three pairs of hungry eyes standing to one side, the headmistress quickly went to the buffet and handed each of us a plate and a mug. The women nearest the table filled our plates with food and poured us some kvass, and we took this scrumptious feast into the dining room, tripping over each other. Yosif proposed a toast, and we three Musketeers narrowly avoided smashing the mugs while clinking them, before joining in the farewell feast. Mother kept topping up our plates as she rushed past us on her way in and out of the kitchen. It was a feast to end all feasts. We were like camels, storing up enough food to last us three days of exotic journeying along the river.

There was so much noise in the next room that we could barely hear each other talk. The women were laughing loudly, telling funny stories over one another.

"That's what alcohol does to people," pontificated Yosif.

"Who?" enquired a puzzled Roman. "Baba-Yaga – the ogress with the bony leg, who eats poo pie," said Yosif slyly. Roman was confused.

"What's poo pie?"

"Don't say 'poo' at the table, you little stinker!"

Seeing that Roman's lip was beginning to quiver, I said to Yosif, "Stop it. You're the one that's like poo on a shoe."

"Shut it. No one's talking to you!" he snapped. "And you're a shit-face!" I retaliated, remembering an insult I had heard in Odessa. He threw his kvass in my face. I hit him on the forehead with my metal spoon, without having first licked it clean. Predictably, a scuffle ensued.

Roman ran to Mother, crying. Laughing, the guests pulled us apart. "Anna Davidovna, here we all were, thinking we'd come to a civilised home and find a boxing club instead. Well, boys, you'd better pull down your pants," said one of the guests, pre-empting the prosecutor, "you're going to get a feel of the strap."

"Since we don't have a strap, there'll be no corporal punishment today," said the second guest, on behalf of the judge, "but little Roman will be the only one to get sweets."

"Citizens, see how sheepish the accused look," said a third one, taking on the role of the defence lawyer.

"They're fully aware of their crime, and begging for forgiveness."

Meeting our mother's reproachful glare, we thought it best not to upset her.

"I'll pay you back later," muttered Yosif as he slinked away.

"Yeah – when pigs fly," I snarled back. The hostess apologised for her sons' rude behaviour, which broke the basic tenets of hospitality. We had spoiled our mother's evening. The next morning, before Nastya arrived with the car, Mother expressed her discontent in no uncertain terms.

"Yesterday, you embarrassed me in front of people who had come as a mark of respect to me, and what did they see? Total disrespect towards me from my very own sons. How can anyone trust me to teach other people's children if I seem unable to control my own? What will they think now? What will they say about our family? Did you even stop to think about that? I don't want to know who started the fight or why. You're both guilty of behaving badly in front of strangers. And because of that, I am not going to speak to you all day. You'll get your food, drink, and a clean towel when you need them. You are not to leave the luggage unattended, except to go to the toilet; you will not touch anything on the barge, and you will not bother anyone with your questions. Do not go anywhere near Roman, and do not talk to each other. As for all the other rules of the move, they're already clear to you. Today, I want each of you to spend some time on his own, giving serious thought to yesterday's behaviour, and to the promise you made father before we left Odessa. And don't bother coming to me with apologies. You should have thought of doing that yesterday, in front of the strangers. I spent eight months trying to establish our reputation as civilised representatives of Ukrainian culture, and you managed to destroy that reputation in just eight seconds. Thanks a lot, children." I don't know about my brother, but I felt totally mortified.

As we drove out of Hussinbach with Nastya, we saw no traces of the animal corpses by the roadside. She explained that they had all been moved in March, and buried in a ditch beyond the woods. Evidently, Anna's conversation with the headmistress had had a positive result. The June landscape we observed was in marked contrast to what we had seen in December. Everything around glowed with the summer hues of luxuriant meadows, the greens of the forests, the bright blue of the sky and dazzling rainbows in the sunlight.

On the way to Marx, our mother asked Nastya if she had any contacts at the wharf, to which she replied that her father-in-law, Kudryavtsev, had given her a written request for help addressed to the manager. The two men had been working for years on bringing farming produce to the Volga region by water.

When we reached the small wharf, Nastya left us in the car while she went looking for the manager. Shortly afterwards, she came back to say that he would be free in about half an hour, and would see us before lunch. Mother said she was willing to pay for the journey by cleaning the inside of the barge. We had more than enough food for three days, since we had taken all our supplies from the house.

After a while, the manager appeared, with Kudryavtsev's letter in his hand. He greeted Nastya with kisses and, extending his arm, invited the women into his office. The three of us stayed behind in the waiting room, sitting in leather armchairs with magazines spread open on our laps, like the best-behaved children in the world. We were even too scared to look at one another, in case that sparked something off.

Finally, our leader appeared, beaming, which meant that everything had been sorted. "Your scamps look like proper little intellectuals," said the manager, referring to us.

On cue, Yosif and I stood to attention, like soldiers. Even Roman, seeing us, climbed off the armchair and stood up straight, though he did not understand why. Nastya burst out laughing, while Mother looked away to hide a smile.

"At ease!" commanded the manager. However, it was an order we didn't understand, so we remained still as statues.

"Sit down and wait here for your mother, while we go and find your pirate ship," he said. Evidently, Anna had told him about our preparations. Nastya kissed her and said goodbye to us.

"Look after your mother," she whispered, "because you wont get another one like her."

At that moment, the manager's elderly secretary came in. Nastya introduced us, then hurried back home. We gathered that the old woman had been brought in to keep an eye on us to make sure we didn't do anything wrong. Evidently, Mother no longer trusted us to remain unattended. So that's how low the bloody Musketeers had fallen. I gave Yosif a dirty look, to which he immediately replied by sticking out his tongue with a grimace. I ignored him, and asked the secretary if I could look at the album about the river fleet. She nodded, and even brought models of river ships for Roman to play with, as long as he promised not to break them.

After finding the captain of one of the moored barges, the manager went for lunch, while Mother came back accompanied by a tall, heavily built sailor. He picked up all our large bags except for the rucksacks and took us to his vessel. At first we thought it would be a long way to walk carrying all that weight, but as we ran around the wharf, we saw that all the barges were moored close to the pier, hidden by vegetation or by nets of leafy branches. We found this breathtakingly beautiful, and eyed one another suspiciously, afraid of letting rip. On board, we were greeted by the captain, who sported a jaunty cap and striped sailor's vest. He saluted us, and Yosif and I returned his salute.

"Welcome aboard Captain Cook's sloop!" he smiled.

"Honoured to be on board, sir," replied the more knowledgeable Yosif on our behalf. The captain explained that it was not the done thing to salute with a bare head. In such cases, you had to cover the top of your head with your left hand. We did as we were told like monkeys in a zoo for three days, much to the amusement of the sailors. It was only as we were leaving that we were let into the secret of the captain's little joke (which was just as well, or we might have returned the compliment with a prank of our own). Too late. No point in closing the stable door once the horse had bolted…

We were allocated a small cabin with two two-storey berths and a window looking out onto the water. We barely had time to arrange the luggage before going to the mess room for a quick bite. After that, Roman went to sleep, while Yosif and I went on deck to explore our vessel. I volunteered to help one of the sailors to wash various sections of the ship with a hose, under his supervision.

Yosif went up to the bridge, where the first mate talked him through all the instruments. Unlike me, my older brother had been fascinated by physics from an early age. The captain declined Mother's offer to pay our way by cleaning, and categorically refused any money. What he did ask for was a signed declaration that she assumed full responsibility for the wellbeing and behaviour of her children on board the ship. From seven in the evening to seven in the morning while the barge was in motion, nobody was to be on deck. If we were not back on board by then, our luggage would be unloaded and we would be left behind. The captain was not authorised to let us off in Kuybyshev, so we would have to leave the ship at Zhiguly, on the opposite bank of the Volga. From there, a steamboat sailed every half hour. We were free to use the mess, except between seven and eight in the morning and five and six in the evening. Anna signed all these terms and conditions, and decided to thank the captain in her own way. With three hours left before departure, we all rushed to the grocery and bought enough steamed milk to fill our magic tin, a string of sweet pretzels and (ask not how), a three-litre bottle of homemade vodka. We were back on board with an easy hour to spare.

After dinner in the mess, we watched the sunset through the cabin window until nightfall. The barge moved smoothly and silently, and the distinctive landscapes of the banks of the Volga floated past. Rocked by the gentle rhythms of the great river, there was something magical about this movement through the darkness. The occasional glow of a sailor's torch only added to the mystery of our voyage. We found our way back to our cabin in the semi-darkness of the safety lights. Our sweet commandant made us all have a warm shower and we fell asleep uncharacteristically early, thoroughly exhausted.

At seven o'clock in the morning, we were woken up by the jolt of the barge as it prepared to moor at Khvalinsk. The shock made us sit up open-mouthed in our berths before we recalled where we were, turned over and went back to sleep.

"Time to get up!" cried Mother, clapping her hands. We pretended to be dead to the world, so she began tickling each of us behind our ears with a goose feather. We tried to wave her away but as soon as we heard that she was going into Khvalinsk on her own, we bounced out of bed, bumping our heads together in the confined space. Mother changed quickly but Yosif and I could not find our pants. Roman was laughing, while Yosif and I rubbed the bumps on our heads.

While the crew were having breakfast, we went to do our morning exercises on deck, under Mother's instructions. The sailors watched us from the mess and giggled, pointing at us. Assuming we had an audience, we showed off even more – but from the warm compliments they paid her afterwards, we soon realised that it was Mother they were admiring, not us. Pigs, I thought, although I couldn't really blame them! Mother had always been elegant and, now, in her sports suit, she looked a real beauty. As men in the making ourselves, we grudgingly understood the feelings of these common sailors, and generously allowed them their suggestive glances.

Khvalinsk turned out to be a small provincial town with a fish processing factory. Mother bought a bundle of carp in the market and promised to cook everyone, including the crew, a fish soup like the one she used to cook in Odessa. Not far from the barge, we spotted a small beach full of small boys. It was hot and we began to whine. Unloading her shopping, Mother promised to come for a swim with us after lunch, on condition that we behaved impeccably. All three of us solemnly swore to come out of the water the minute she called. As the time for cooking lunch approached, we grabbed the necessary vegetables and rushed back to the barge, where everyone except for the officer on the deck was still snoring. While the cook busied herself in the kitchen preparing Odessa fish soup, Yosif and I sunbathed on deck, and Roman took his afternoon nap. The mouth-watering smells of Mother's cooking wafted across the entire jetty. Even the captain, awoken by these olfactory delights, decided to investigate in the mess. He was pleasantly surprised to hear that the fish soup was intended for the whole crew but could not understand why Mother had gone to so much trouble and expense. As though she had read his thoughts, Anna said, "I hope, after you've all had lunch, there'll be some left for my children." The captain smiled and thanked her. His refugee passenger told him we were all going to the beach, and would be back by six.

The Volga is a very wide – 1,000–1,500 metre – navigable river, and dangerously deep in parts. The beach was in the lagoon, where the water is waist-high, and therefore safe for children. Signs stated that swimming in the river itself was forbidden by law. Even so, Anna decided to check the depth of the lagoon for herself before allowing us to jump in. She and Roman splashed about at the shallow end, while my brother and I dived in and out like a couple of seals that had finally found new water. Thanks to Roman, who stubbornly refused to leave the water, Yosif and I had enormous fun, both physically and emotionally. After all, who knew when next we would have such a lucky break?

Mother beamed as we tumbled onto our beds later, exhausted but happy. She made no secret of her joy at seeing her children so enjoying themselves. She felt it was but small reward for the sufferings they had endured over the past twelve months – and also those that were probably to come between now and the end of the war. Those two hours on the beach flew like as many minutes. Yosif read, while I admired our mother. Even in that modest swimsuit, she looked not like a dowdy mother of three, but the star of a silent movie in an old-fashioned dress.

"Misha, what are you staring at me like that for?" she joked. "Don't you recognise me? It's me – your own mother, from Odessa!" Good God. It had been such a long time since I had seen her simply relax with us. Roman could not stand our mother's attention being focused on me, so he climbed up on her lap, and jealously shielded her from my sight.

"Onwards, Musketeers!" sounded the familiar command. As we came closer to the barge, we heard someone softly singing a coachman's song. The elderly crew – over sixty, so beyond fighting age – were now relaxing, having eaten copious amounts of Mother's fish soup. When they saw us, they stopped singing and began thanking the passenger for the soup. In reply, she put her hand on her heart, and asked them to continue their song. However, they timidly shook their heads.

So then Annushka, the first mate, intoned the old folk song *Karobushka*, and, encouraged, the sailors joined in chorus to sing the familiar tune. The captain could not believe his eyes and ears. Astounded, Yosif and Roman sat down on the deck, by the window. Standing with my arm around my mother, I sang along a tone lower, as we had been taught to do at music school. There was a protracted pause at the end of the song. Everyone waited to see the captain's reaction. He slowly stood up, sighed and began applauding. I had not heard such a loud standing ovation for a long time. It was their way of saying goodbye to us.

I can't describe our surprise when, the next morning, the captain dropped us not in Zhiguly, as previously agreed, but in Kuybyshev. This was as a token of thanks for the song the previous day. He didn't yet know of the surprise thank you gift that awaited him in his cabin, from the three young pirates and their lady commander.

Weighed down by rucksacks and string bags, we came out of the jetty onto the square, where the tram was on its way back into the town centre. The duty policeman gave us the address of the nearest evacuation point. Being highly experienced by now, we found the address easily and walked into the building as though we were coming home. Not many refugees had arrived that morning. We were dealt with according to protocol.

When our turn came, we were informed that there was no accommodation available in the city itself. Given a choice of options suitable for a family of four, Mother picked Zhiguly, funnily enough. This was obviously where we were destined to end our wartime wanderings. They confirmed to Mother all the financial assistance for food and accommodation. They gave the necessary information for her search for our father, and tickets for the transport of evacuees. We had two hours to wait, which gave us enough time for lunch and a quick tour of this large city. There was no hint of war here, and everything looked quiet. We were driven with another family to the jetty and, from there we crossed the Volga by steamboat to the village of Vypolzovo in the Zhiguly district. It took us ten minutes to drive twelve kilometres. They were expecting us at the Village Council, and we were promptly allocated fully furnished and equipped homes.

We were so worn out by the constant running away that we were initially unable to appreciate the comforts we had been so unexpectedly given by a twist of fate. Built from solid timber, the house had most probably been an important person's second home before the war. They must have lived in Kuybyshev, coming to the country to commune with nature on their days off. The last wooden planks were being taken off the boarded-up doors and windows as we drove up in our noisy jeep.

Our new administrator, Auntie Dusya, led us ceremoniously into the semi-dark house. She opened the inner blinds, gradually letting more and more light flood into every room, and warned us not to damage the expensive furniture or block the toilets. Mother promised that she would keep everything clean and orderly in this magic abode, throwing us self-explanatory looks. In reply, we innocently raised our eyebrows and nodded in agreement, while stroking the expensive velvet upholstery with our filthy hands.

Again, we were pleasantly surprised to find that wicker baskets with food had been left on the kitchen table: bread, milk, potatoes, eggs, pumpkin and other treasures. We were about to devour this appetising still life but froze in mid-reach on hearing a familiar command. Yosif and I calculatingly changed the course of our hands, redirecting them from the table to scratching the backs of our heads. Roman glanced inquisitively from us to Mother, not understanding why we couldn't eat these tempting delights. Our commander indicated the sink where Yosif and I were already washing our hands. Auntie Dusya smiled and nodded approvingly.

"Anna, you have very well-behaved boys," she said.

"Oh, yes," Mother answered quickly. "Sometimes, on special days..."

While we devoured the bread and milk, Dusya showed our mother around indoors and outdoors. There was a small but convenient garden with suitable sheds, dried flowers in vases and in the flower-beds, a rusty bicycle – everything spoke of a wealthy owner who had not visited his luxurious possessions for a long time. At the back of the house, there was a 100-square-metre vegetable garden which led down to the family bathhouse, which was small but had a tall pipe for the sauna. The vegetable patch was overgrown with weeds, and over-ripe fruit was lying on the ground, waiting for the owner. Dusya offered help in clearing the vegetable garden and sowing new seeds but Mother was half-hearted about this prospect. She said she had to look for work to pay for our winter clothes and to stock up on food.

Chapter 4

THE UPS AND DOWNS OF LIFE IN ZHIGULY

After settling in, we explored all the entertainment possibilities of the shed and store rooms, where we discovered (as well as the bicycle) a wheelbarrow for carrying wood – and little Roman. Although he was delighted by this exciting new means of transport, we all got a stern ticking off from Mother when she saw the effects of our little game on his trousers, which were liberally caked in manure and torn by protruding nails. Although bare-bottomed while Mother whisked away the impressively disreputable garment for cleaning and repair, Roman didn't cry for long. Yosif set about driving the offending nails firmly into the barrow and swung the heavy hammer painfully onto his thumb in the process. I took great pains to hose down Roman's new carriage, and of course 'accidentally' caught my gawping brothers with the water jet. As she scrubbed the liberally soiled trousers in the kitchen sink, Mother heard hysterical screams shatter the usual tranquillity of the garden and rushed out to see Roman, stark naked, being sprayed with cold water from the hose as it thrashed around unattended while Yosif and I yet again determinedly wrestled each other across the garden, to the obvious detriment of our newly laundered clothes.

This incident marked the official inauguration of the Three Musketeers' Club, whose members were on this occasion punished by being locked up in the house for the rest of the day. Roman constantly twitched during his after-lunch nap, no doubt dreaming he was still being doused with holy water. Yosif and I sat far apart from each other, leafing through ancient magazines until Mother finished her chores and summoned us both to her presence for a serious talking-to.

In the parlour, we saw the familiar envelopes of photographs, receipts and money, all carefully laid out on the table. We stared, genuinely at a loss as to why all these papers were on display. Mother stared into our eyes for an uncomfortably long time, assessing our ability to understand what she was about to say at our young age. She sighed, and spoke quietly but firmly.

"I don't want to hear any more arguments between you, or see any more fighting. You must, repeat, must put a stop to them. Just look at the people next door. They have children your age who help their mothers around the house. They look after the animals. They work in the vegetable gardens. They clean, they cook, they do everything they can. And that's the kind of help I need now – more than ever before, unless you want me to collapse."

We both paid attention. We realised this was not another emotional maternal rant, but something new, that her voice and her eyes were conveying something momentous. "I know perfectly well that you're only ten and twelve years old," she continued after another deep sigh, "And, judging by the way you behave to each other, you're nowhere near ready to face the trials that your father told you about. Nevertheless, you must understand the critical financial situation we're in. It's vitally important that you know and remember this, and take responsibility for yourselves. You must start behaving properly, both at home and in front of strangers, and start taking moral responsibility for our family and our future. If anything were to happen to me, you must be able to survive, for my sake and your father's. Do I make myself clear?"

I could tell that Mother didn't want to spell out all her misgivings about what the future held. Her warning about hardships to come reminded me of father's parting words to us in Odessa. We realised that there were things she had deliberately left unsaid. My head spun in a whirlwind of dark thoughts. What is Mother preparing us for, exactly? What are these papers doing out on the table? Is something really going to happen to her? Is she trying to warn us that we'll be left alone, without her? Does she want us to know where everything is, just in case?

As though reading our anxious minds, she picked up one of the envelopes. "This is our entire month's allowance, which – even if we're extremely frugal – will last two or three weeks at the most. Our Odessa money ran out long ago. We have nothing of value left to sell. Unlike the neighbours, we don't have a garden full of vegetables ready to eat. I've tried finding work in the local school, the hospital and the kindergarten, but without success. The village council has promised to clear the vegetable garden and plant some potatoes, carrots and beetroot, which should be ready before the winter. But to have any crops for us to harvest in three months' time, the late planted seeds will all have to be regularly watered and kept clear of weeds between now and then. Even between us, we're not physically capable of doing it all. The only way I can earn enough to clothe us and buy what you need for school is by going to work on a building site fifteen kilometres away. That means I'll have to spend five nights a week over there, in a women's hostel. Roman will have to go to kindergarten as a boarder five nights a week, and we'll spend Saturdays and Sundays together. Now, how do you two feel about sleeping alone in this big house, and looking after yourselves?"

We listened open-mouthed, unable to believe our ears. Incredulous smiles were our initial reaction, on the hopeful assumption that her words must be yet another maternal ploy to scare us into obedience. However, as we read the profound sadness on her face, we gradually realised that we faced a stark and very real choice: either we dutifully accepted the enormous sacrifice our mother was making for our sake, or we would not have the food and warmth to survive the bitter winter ahead in this magnificent house. As usual, Yosif mumbled something grumpily, but our commander's calm, steely tone hushed his muttered protestations.

"I knew you'd understand, and I'm sure you'll do the right thing. As the wise men from the east say, always choose the lesser of two evils." I nodded in agreement and, ignoring Yosif's hostile glare, sought her permission to ask a few questions. When exactly will we start living on our own, without adult supervision? Where should we go in case of emergency? Which one of us will be responsible for what during the week? Just as I was about to voice these concerns, our protector stopped me with a raised hand and explained that she had already thought of these things. In fact, she had written down lists of our respective tasks and responsibilities on separate sheets of paper. Yosif fidgeted nervously on his chair, but she paid no attention.

Mother's tasks:

1. Take Roman to kindergarten on Monday mornings and pick him up again on Friday evenings

2. Clean the kitchen and toilet, wash and iron, bathe the children, mend clothes, etc.

3. Do the accounts for all school and household expenses, and discuss the week's timetable

Yosif's tasks:

1. Pay bills, buy and prepare food

2. Keep in touch with Auntie Dusya, next-door neighbours, etc.

3. Be responsible for fire appliances: stove, paraffin lamp, fireplace, etc.

Misha's tasks:

1. Wash dishes after every meal, clean the house and garden

2. Look after the vegetable patch: water, weed, trim bushes, etc.

3. Visit Roman at kindergarten every day before dinnertime

Having examined our duties, my brother and I exchanged glances. Our days of carefree childhood were clearly over. When Roman woke up and called out for Mother, we picked up and read her own personal list of tasks for her days off, which she had left on the table. She was taking a lot upon herself. Yosif nodded towards the door, and we went outside. Sitting on logs opposite each other outside the shed, we studied our lists and, for the first time in our lives, tried to comply with our mother's wishes and discuss our future duties without arguing. But Yosif, unhappy about relinquishing his freedom, soon got onto his hobbyhorse.

"We should've gone to Tashkent, where half the people from Odessa were evacuated to."

"No point in bringing that up now," I interrupted. "It's too late – there's no money left to move anywhere else. The Zhiguly Mountains are behind us, and the Volga ahead of us. I guess we're stuck here till the end of the war." I tried flattery. "You're two years older than me, and you've read lots more books than me. Can't you see what's happening to Mummy? She's like a cornered dog with three pups. If we don't help her now, she'll be done for."

He stood up and turned to me aggressively. "Don't you lecture me about what to do, you snotty little oik!"

Instinctively reaching out for a log behind me, I snarled back: "You bastard, touch me one more time and I'll smash your book-filled head in with this. So you'd better sit down, you piece of shit! Let's sort this out without arguing, like we promised." (My longstanding friendship with gypsy neighbours in Odessa had done much to expand my vocabulary.) "We'll go back indoors. If you're not happy with something on these lists, then go and suggest an alternative to Mummy. Just don't whinge. You and I can swap jobs if you want, I don't care. I just want to look after her health and not waste time on stupid fights."

Yosif sat quietly, frowning at me as though I had just stolen something from him, or mortally offended him. What he heard in my threatening tone of voice stopped him from lashing back in return, and made him – Yosif, the man of the house – reflect on the fate of our family. Nevertheless, a peaceful brotherly talk did not take place. I often tried to understand why Yosif behaved with such unreasonable selfishness, but could only think of one possible reason. Our parents' first child, David, died of meningitis. Yosif had been diagnosed with a heart problem and so, fearing the loss of a second child, Mother had cosseted him from an early age. Being constantly worried about his health had obviously impaired my brother's sense of independence, his natural immunity and survival instinct. He was compensating for his own insecurities.

I remember our parents discussing my tearaway tendencies, saying it was too late to change me, and all that could be done was instil me with discipline and self-control. I had a bad feeling that my brother would find some excuse not to carry out his jobs, and that sooner or later I'd end up doing the work for the both of us, as usual. When Yosif went to the village council library, I shared my concerns with Mother. This upset her greatly and, after saying nothing for a long time, she suddenly turned and asked me what I would do in her shoes. At first, I was thrown by having my question answered by another, but then summoned my courage.

"I just don't know. I guess that when I have a family of my own, I'll try to work out a compromise – a situation where everyone wins."

She gave a sad laugh. "My dearest Misha, you're a bit too quick for a ten-year-old. I sometimes worry about your future. Where do you get all this stuff? Come on, tell me. Is it at the library, or reading 'Popular Proverbs and Sayings' in the magazine? They're easy enough to remember…" She hesitated. "As for Yosif, I have my doubts that he'll carry out all his jobs, too. That's why I've arranged for Auntie Dusya to come every evening at six o'clock after work to help Yosif make dinner – for the first few days, at least. There's tinned meat and fish in the cupboard, and some macaroni, rice, buckwheat and root vegetables for soup. Misha, darling, I think you're perfectly capable of cooking something simple, too. I saw Klava teach you when we were in Zarnitza."

"Yes, but it's unfair to give all the work to one son just because the other one's too selfish and lazy to do any!" I burst out. Mother threw her hands up and suddenly turned towards the window. She seemed to be wiping away tears with her apron. I realised that I shouldn't have flown off the handle like that, however justifiably. I hugged her from behind and pressed my cheek against her back. I apologised for my outburst and promised to do anything she said as long as she stopped crying. That, however, only moved her even more deeply. I ran out into the garden and, fighting back my own tears, I grabbed the rickety bicycle and rode into the village so furiously that the chain fell off. I kept trying to imagine what I would do in the mother's place, but could find no solution. I was wheeling the bike back home when I heard someone call from a neighbouring house.

"Hey – you! Cavalryman! Stop right there! What happened to your horse – lost a shoe?"

At first, I couldn't work out where the unfamiliar voice was coming from, but then I noticed the hunched figure of an old man ambling towards the gate. I greeted him. Tipping his cap slightly, he enquired in a croaking voice, "You're the son of that new Ukrainian refugee, aren't you?"

"That's right," I replied off-handedly. He'd probably start asking lots of questions now, and I wasn't in the mood. I wondered how I could extricate myself without causing offence.

"Your bike looks older than me, son, but I can make it look younger in my workshop."

"I've got no money, granddad," I replied irritably.

The old man didn't give up so easily. "I don't give a toss about your money, boy. I just need to chew the fat with someone every now and then. Both my sons are at war, and I'm left here all alone – and getting blonder by the day," he smiled, indicating his white locks. "You live just around the corner, in Slavka Filin's house, right?"

"Uh-huh," I nodded. The old chap had probably lost his marbles from spending too much time alone, I thought.

"Well then, leave your lame steed with me here and you can pick it up tomorrow, fully restored to health." I was so astounded I couldn't say or do anything. Was he joking, or what?

"So, new boy, what's your name?"

"Mikhail. Yours?"

"I'm just old Sidor. So now we're acquainted. See you tomorrow, my boy!"

"OK. 'Bye then, granddad."

As I approached home, I caught a whiff of Mother's garlicky borscht and quickened my step. After perfunctorily rinsing my hands, I sat at the table and wished my brothers *bon appétit*, but got no reply. Our commander was busy over the stove and Roman was licking his painted wooden spoon. Yosif, between mouthfuls, casually threw down the gauntlet.

"So – where's our one and only bike, then?"

Mother's back suddenly tensed. Expecting a fight, Roman dropped his spoon in the bowl, splashing borscht onto the table. Without blinking, I blurted: "Sold it for fifty kopeks."

Hastily, I tried to remember how much that was in roubles. Mother giggled. Yosif sniggered hollowly. Innocently, Roman asked, "Is that enough to buy a horse?"

Much to his surprise, we all collapsed in hysterics, prompting Yosif to swallow his food the wrong way. In the ensuing coughing fit, he violently expelled a spurt of the aromatic purple liquid, splashing everyone at the table. Shaking with helpless laughter, Mother held a bowl full of borscht perilously close to me and I slipped away from the table to avoid being inadvertently baptised by my favourite dish. The more Roman hammered furiously on the table with his spoon, demanding an answer to his question about the horse, the more we laughed. The whole scene was like something out of a slapstick comedy film, except that it was far from silent. Sitting on the couch, I wondered what our poor neighbours were making of this racket. They must think it a madhouse, overrun by barbarians…

As if echoing my thoughts, the usual drama was then played out at the kitchen table. While Mother busied herself with pots and pans over the stove, her back to us. Yosif had stopped coughing and became suddenly irritated at Roman drumming on the table. He snatched the painted wooden spoon out of his hand and hit the little drummer on the forehead with it. Naturally, the would-be timpanist screamed loud enough for the entire village to hear, confirming our presence to our neighbours in no uncertain terms. Angrily, our Bagheera sprang to the defence of her young cub. She skilfully disarmed the culprit, snatched the spoon out of his hand and struck Yosif on the head with it so hard that the spoon broke.

"But what have I done?" protested Yosif plaintively.

"What you've done is disobey my explicit instructions to keep your hands to yourself. And that, my boy, is what it feels like to be hit by someone bigger and stronger than you are!"

"Hares may pull dead lions by the beard…" I remarked slyly, while trying to comfort Roman by giving him back his broken spoon.

"I'll sort you out later," muttered Yosif, rubbing the bump on his head. Before I could open my mouth to retaliate, Mother finally placed the long-awaited bowl of borscht in front of me and silenced me with a single glance. "Yosif, leave the table and stay in your room for the rest of the evening. You and I will have a private talk tomorrow. Good night!"

This was a humiliating punishment for Yosif. Mother seemed determined to show the Musketeers who was boss. She often used to do the same with me in Odessa, as I was considered the most disobedient child in the family. I couldn't remember her ever punishing Yosif at all, let alone so publicly. He was always the exemplar of good behaviour, a diligent pupil at school, and he never got involved in street fights. He was like a houseplant.

I, on the other hand, was often punished and sometimes even spanked; Mother would beat the dust from the seat of my trousers. But it didn't stop me breaking garden windows with my football, or jumping on and off the steps of the trams that sped past our house, or giving other boys bloody noses (and returning home with my own features rearranged as a consequence). My relatives and teachers warned Mother several times that I was so fond of strong sensations and risky adventures that I would never die a natural death. I just agreed with them and resigned myself to my fate with a casual, "So be it."

World war, however, changed the innocence of childhood as well as society in general. It altered children's consciousness, their instinctive behaviour and the way they related to each other. It was naive of us to assume that our long deprivation of peace and stability would end here, in our idyllic new home in this romantic district of Zhiguly. Two years was the nearest we got to permanence, and our circumstances were far from idyllic.

The week after allocating our tasks, Mother started work on the building site, satisfied with the programme she had put in place. Before leaving, she bought the food we would need from the market and cooked a huge pot of potatoes and beetroot and a mountain of blinis, buckwheat porridge and hard-boiled eggs. She worried nevertheless, although everything had also been arranged with Auntie Dusya.

The first week went more or less smoothly. Yosif checked the post office and shopped at the village store, and reheated the pre-cooked food. I did the washing up, kept the house clean and visited Roman before dinner every day. I spent my spare time working on the vegetable patch, and after the private talk with Mother, Yosif took it upon himself to water the vegetables every day. Auntie Dusya came to check that we were all right every evening between six and seven. I don't know what our commander told Yosif before she left, but he stopped sulking like a prima donna. He tried hard to be responsible about keeping the house and the garden tidy, and helped me weed the garden and so on. Not being a believer in miracles, I kept expecting him to turn – once bitten, twice shy, as they say.

In the evenings we played chess. We had found a set in the pantry behind the samovar, and after replacing the missing pieces with cardboard cut-outs, we spent many happy hours battling each other on the board. Yosif introduced me to many of the game's tactics and strategies with remarkable patience. At exactly ten o'clock every evening, Dusya would come back, turn out the lamps, wait for us to lock the door with its heavy wooden bolt, wish us goodnight and return home. At the time, we couldn't understand why this was thought necessary, as it just gave her one more thing to worry about. Later, Mother patiently explained to us that all women have a maternal instinct; those with no children of their own find another outlet for these inborn feelings and urges – sometimes even with cats, dogs or other domestic animals. In this case, here were three children in need of nurturing, and childless Dusya was ready to give her heart to them unconditionally.

The first week kept us so busy with our chores that we almost didn't notice Friday come upon us. That evening, we stood on the porch to welcome our mother and Roman in our Musketeer attire – that is, with aluminium saucepans on our heads as helmets, dustbin lids on our left arms as shields and, in our right hand, large ladles as swords. The effect was completed by wearing kitchen aprons front and back as tabards and cloaks. As they approached, we banged our swords on our shields to welcome them as honoured guests. Alarmed, our immediate neighbours flung open their windows, only to slam them shut again, laughing at our masquerade. Roman shrieked with excitement; tears welled in Mother's eyes. My brother and I staged a well-rehearsed duel.

Old Sidor hobbled over to the site of the fracas. "Hey, Mikhail, why didn't you come and pick up your steed? I reshod him ages ago…"

Mother replied before I could. "Thank you so much for taking care of my boys," she said.

"No thanks needed, my dear. I did it with all my heart. And if you ever need a handyman around the place, I'm your man. God bless you and your home!"

Mother stood rooted on the spot, astounded, until the old man had limped away out of sight around the corner. We three also kept quiet, reluctant to break the spell. Finally, our wise Bagheera turned to us and excitedly said, "Just look at that, children. Look and remember – even a sick old man can have a heart big enough to want to help perfect strangers without wanting anything in return."

The next morning, when I brought the bicycle back from Sidor, everybody rushed out into the road to admire how a rusty piece of old junk had been magically transformed into a shiny new machine. Repaired, cleaned, painted and oiled, it looked a real beauty. He had replaced the bent back wheel and made a seat for Roman on the frame out of a cushion and some sacking, He had also attached a basket on the back, a small lamp on the handlebars and a tyre pump under the saddle. We were delighted.

Mother stood smiling on the porch, lost in her own thoughts. 'Lord, look at how my boys have grown up during this difficult year. Am I wrong to be so strict with them? No, I'm not – it's my job to make them into proper men, especially as their father isn't around... God! What am I saying? Am I trying to bring bad luck? Stupid woman – I'm losing my reason, with all this constant fear...'

We yelled out for our anxious commander to come and see Yosif cycling down the street, with Roman on board. Suddenly wrenched out of her reverie, she initially reacted with a cry of "Be careful! Don't drop him!" but then, thinking better of it, she applauded Yosif for his kindness to her youngest. Seeing my knowing smile, she wisely decided to leave us to it, pleased with the result of her talk with us about family behaviour. That evening, Dusya came with the monthly allocation of money and they had a long discussion about something or other in the kitchen, behind closed doors. Then Dusya left, upset, without even wishing us goodnight.

On Sunday, Yosif went to the library first thing in the morning. Roman was on the makeshift swing in the garden and I helped Mother with the housework. She kept wincing and clutching her stomach – unfamiliar gestures that worried me. When I asked, she just gave a forced smile, and said it was just physical strain from working on the building site – that in a week or so, her muscles would have got used to it, and all would be well. Telling her I had always wanted to learn how to wash floors, I relieved her of the mop and neatly manoeuvred the wet cloth around the table and chair legs, making her laugh.

"Misha darling, it's a mop, not a sword," she said. "Remember, we promised Auntie Dusya we'd take good care of the owner's furniture." But I was in full swing. I finished washing the parlour floor as fast as I could, gave the hall a wipe, and then rode astride the mop into the garden. There, I performed an excellent impression of a Red Indian hunting on horseback, to excited cries of encouragement from Roman. Elegant even in distress, the lady of the house stood on the porch, forcing a smile and clutching at her stomach while I continued clowning about.

At the end of her second week on the building site, Mother failed to return home. On Friday evening, it was Dusya who brought Roman home from kindergarten instead, and broke the news that our mother was seriously ill and had been taken to hospital for an urgent operation. As she put the food away in the kitchen, she tried to explain the situation as calmly as she could, but her voice was trembling.

"But what exactly is wrong with Mother, then?" asked Yosif.

Dusya hesitated. "She... she got a prolapse on the building site." Uncomprehending, we waited for an explanation. "Because of all the heavy lifting, her bowels... have collapsed," she blurted out, clearly alarmed.

"So that's why she kept clutching at her stomach last Sunday!" I exclaimed.

"Shut up, you idiot! No one asked you."

Dusya immediately raised her hands between us, putting a stop to the fight before it had even begun. "Boys, now is not the time for fights. The best you can do is look after yourselves and take care of each other. Yosif – you must act as both father and Mother to your brothers. That's how it's always been done in families. I'll take Roman home with me on his days off kindergarten, and you two take care of everything here, as you promised your mother you would."

"When's she coming home, then?" whimpered Roman.

"Soon, son, don't worry. You'll be all right staying with me."

Dusya collected Roman's clothes, toys and rucksacks. Yosif loaded everything on the bike, put his little brother on the saddle and they went to the unfamiliar house. As she was saying goodbye, Dusya tried to tell me something but couldn't. She pressed me against her, shaking with sobs, kissed my head and followed after my brothers. I stared after them for a long time, as though in a trance, sitting on the earth mound by the gate. Stunned by recent events, we were in no condition to appreciate the gravity of the situation – certainly not so soon. All I felt was a profound emptiness, both inside and out.

When Yosif returned on the bicycle, he found me still sitting on the mound. He put his hand on my shoulder and suggested we had dinner. What a miraculous transformation, I thought. He stood before me, silent. I wondered if this enemy-brother of mine would indeed turn into a protective older brother. Judging by appearances, Dusya must have bolstered his pride on their trek to her house. In any case, I couldn't swallow a single morsel. The food stuck in my throat.

Gradually, the situation became clearer as we worked out what must have happened. During their animated discussion in the kitchen about our future, Mother had probably wanted to avoid losing her temporary job at the building site, while Dusya refused to accept responsibility for three children left to their own devices. Mother must have overestimated both her own strength as well as her children's independence. She had bitten off more than even she could chew.

'Teach' back in Odessa had been right to say that in any enterprise, self-confidence is half the battle. The other half, though, is down to luck – favourable circumstances. As our former nanny in Odessa, Sasha, used to say: "You won't get far on enthusiasm alone. Bread is baked by the sweat of your brow, and not just sweet words."

So now we had to work the vegetable patch regularly, and dig out the potatoes on time. Dusya kept asking us about them. When we asked why potatoes were so important, she explained that not only could they be a substitute for bread, but they could also be easily sold in town to get money for clothes. When our immediate neighbours heard that the children in Filin's house were effectively parentless, they began dropping off fruit, pickles, pies and other food. We'd find a string bag swinging modestly from the handle of our front door, without even knowing whom we should thank. It made us feel very much out of our depth. Either way, it was good to know that our fellow villagers were concerned about our welfare, and their kindness eventually persuaded me that Russians are by nature tender-hearted folk who prefer not to brag about their good deeds.

As promised, Mother was brought home on the Saturday in a covered ambulance emblazoned with a painted red cross. The neighbours opposite opened their windows without bothering to conceal their curiosity. The woman driver and the nurse gently helped their patient out, stood her up and slowly walked her into the house, supporting her under each arm. We rushed out to greet our mother, but were stopped by her sturdy protectors, who warned us that she had to be treated with great care after such a complicated operation, and that unless she had at least a week's complete rest to recover, she would end up back in hospital. While the driver settled her patient on the couch, the nurse laid out all the medicines on the table and instructed us on how they should be administered. Addressing us formally, like adults, they both stated in unison that we were not to allow Mother to lift anything heavy or make any sudden movements, and that her health depended on us. We nodded in silence. A familiar smile lit up Mother's pale face as she thanked the two women for taking care of her.

When our commander eventually asked how her Musketeers had coped in her absence, we interrupted one another with reports on the vegetable patch, the mysterious bags of food, our preparations for school and so on. She was dismayed to hear about the food from unknown sources, and told us never to touch food given by strangers in future. "Even animals are careful," she said. "A person with honourable intentions has no need to hide. Otherwise, how do you know the food isn't poisoned?"

My brother and I were rather discouraged by this particular piece of wisdom. When we asked for details of what had actually happened to her, she replied curtly that she had developed a prolapse through carrying heavy loads, then quickly added, "And now, children, I need to rest. It was a long ambulance journey."

My brother and I duly walked away and went into the garden, behind the shed, to the spot where we traditionally discussed family issues.

"What do you think?" I asked Yosif after a brief silence.

"I think our Bagheera miscalculated again. She obviously didn't expect the work on the building site to be quite so physically strenuous, or realise that we're not really up to living independently."

I nodded my agreement with his analysis so far.

"What's your problem?" he asked, suspicious even of my assent. "In chess terms, it's what's known as overestimating your own abilities and underestimating your opponent's. That's probably what the row with Dusya was about."

133

As usual, Yosif strove to assert his intellectual superiority. Although I was surprised that we agreed so much, I was still determined to prove to him that I could also hold my own. The aim, in any case, had to be to support Mother's struggle to secure our wellbeing. I sighed deeply.

"I agree with you in principle, but in chess terms, maybe her act of self-sacrifice might put Mother in a better position with local employers, and make them more likely to want to help the family of a serving soldier. After all, she was only trying to keep us from harm. We all make mistakes," I continued with pensive air. "But the fact is, both of us found it hard to manage without Mother this last week – emotionally hard as well as physically hard. We've just got to help her get well again so she can get her panther instincts back again. We have to do it not just out of love, but from a purely selfish point of view to ensure our future freedom, comfort and safety," I concluded.

Yosif stared at me in disbelief. "Get you! When did you turn so wise?"

"Same time as you," I replied with false modesty. "I suppose if I hang around you long enough, some things are bound to rub off." We gave each other a self-satisfied hand slap.

"All right," said Yosif. "Let's follow the same programme all next week, until September, and give Mum a chance to get back on her feet again."

"Exactly. Let's show her what her defenceless little puppies are really capable of. We'll take it in turns to look after her all week, OK? We'll take turns after lunch."

"Right. Let's get to work!" said Yosif, sealing our agreement. We returned to the kitchen, where Mother was already rattling the kettle. Exchanging a glance, we rushed over and my brother carefully took the kettle from her hands and passed it to me. He persuaded her to put her weight on his shoulder and led her back into the parlour. "Boys, am I dreaming, or is this for real?" she asked.

"Madam, you'll soon get your answer. In the meantime, not a step without support – nurse's orders."

On the Sunday before classes were supposed to resume, Yosif and I cycled to the school with empty rucksacks. Although I barely came up to his chin in height, I was stronger, so we often swapped places – I rode on the handlebars and he on the saddle, and vice versa. With the extra weight, the tyres often needed pumping up.

We were warmly welcomed at the school. First, we were introduced to the headmistress, Vassilissa Yegorovna, then the deputy headmistress, Agrippina Markovna, took us to our respective classes – Yosif to the fifth grade and me to the third. I vainly protested that having already completed the third grade the previous year, I wanted to go into the fourth. However, on checking our files, the deputy headmistress confirmed that at my age I should be in the third grade. She said that they would move me up if I got bored, which I took as a personal insult.

Yosif smirked spitefully, gloating at his newfound superiority. As I followed him and the deputy headmistress down the corridor, I was itching to kick him, but resisted the temptation. The face of an old gypsy in Odessa suddenly flashed before me. She had told me more than once that because my astrological sign was Taurus, I always tended to attack my opponent without evaluating him first, like the proverbial bull in a china shop. I had to learn to control myself, especially in these new circumstances.

There were twenty pupils in my class, all noisily chatting to one another – the girls on one side, the boys opposite. I greeted the elderly teacher with an automatic bow. She smiled kindly and asked if I came from a theatrical family. The deputy handed her my file and wished me success in my studies. Zinayda Borisovna, my new 'teach', leafed through my papers and raised her eyebrows. "Didn't you complete the third grade last year?"

"Yes I did," I agreed resentfully, "But the headmistress put me with you because of my age, not my level."

Zinayda Borisovna looked discouraged. "Very well, then. Stay with us for a month, then we'll see. All right?"

I nodded. Everything about this woman suggested kindness and warmth. She had a nice smile, and I was enchanted by her velvety voice. She told me to take a full set of the third grade textbooks laid out in stacks on one of the tables, and a pile of exercise books from the other. I also had to copy the week's class timetable from the blackboard, and be at school at eight the following morning.

As I waited downstairs by the bicycle for Yosif, I watched the other pupils, some of them probably in the same grade as me. They too studied the new foreigner, as we were called in the village. The truth is, we not only looked different – Mother trimmed our hair herself – but we walked and talked differently. But I knew from my experience of the Stalingrad evacuation camp and at the Hussinbach school that social barriers would dissolve after a month or so, even for Yosif, who was not quite so sociable and forthcoming with strangers. His reserve and natural wariness made it harder for him to make new friends or to find a chess partner. He preferred the safe company of the characters in books, or to study both sides of chess openings on his own.

Yosif's schoolbooks couldn't all fit into his rucksack, so I had to stuff a couple into my own. We put both loads on the handlebars and into the basket at the back and pushed the overloaded bike on foot through the whole village. I wished Mother could see Yosif dragging his feet, his face contorted with rage. "Tomorrow, I'm cycling to school. You can find your own way there!" he declared provocatively. Same old, same old, I thought. I was dying to spit in his face, but the old gypsy stopped me, again: "What are you – a camel, spitting like that? Keep your mouth shut!"

I moved away sharply, leaving the steering to him. That was obviously the outcome Yosif had been expecting, because he immediately jumped onto the saddle and rode off, leaving me to walk half the journey home alone. I was so incensed my mouth fell open. My athletic brother, though, had clearly forgotten about the two heavy rucksacks swinging from side to side on the handlebars and in the basket. The unstable extra weight soon made him lose his balance, and he came crashing down on the dusty road, the bike and its cargo landing on top of him. I was a bit alarmed when I first saw him fall, but then thought to myself, cruelly: as Sasha used to say, that's divine retribution for trying to leave me behind, you bastard!

Yosif's piercing yelp of pain and humiliation brought several our fellow villagers to their windows, sleepily peering out after being so rudely awoken from their Sunday afternoon nap. While I helped to disentangle the casualty, dragging the bicycle off him, a kind-hearted woman came out with a flask of water and some herbal disinfectant. She gently bathed the rider's grazed knee and elbow, smeared a thick layer of herb poultice on his cuts and croaked, "Stop crying, lad. You'll be good as new in time for your wedding, I promise."

"Thanks," muttered Yosif, somewhat revived. I wheeled the bicycle the rest of the way home. As colourful as a parrot, all red and green, my shamefaced brother held on to the basket at the back. No words were exchanged, but Yosif knew exactly what I was thinking as he limped along, his head down. Stung by the humiliation of it all, he hoped that I would pause for a rest without having to wound his pride further by asking me himself. But I kept on pushing the bike, making it clear that I had no intention of being delayed any longer. Unkind as it seems, I reminded myself that he too had behaved abominably, riding on ahead without me, abandoning me on my own in the middle of the road. I was curious to know how he would have explained his selfishness to our mother; she would certainly have forced him to go back for me, or come to get me herself. She would have taught him a lesson. When in Rome, do as the Romans do.

On reaching home, I had to interrupt my musings. I gulped lunch in a rush and went to the garden to try and solve the school transport issue for the next day. Yosif's crash had twisted the back wheel of the bike, the handlebars were misaligned and the chain had come off, so I took the unprepossessing wreck around the corner to Old Sidor. As usual, he sat dozing on the earth mound. On hearing the familiar creaks and rattles, he woke up with a start.

"It's you, Misha! What, more mishaps with your steed?"

"I'm so sorry, we had an accident. My brother and I went to enrol at the school and we both fell off on the way. As you know, the school's on the other side of the village – it takes at least half an hour on foot, especially when you're carrying a heavy rucksack as well."

"All right, all right – spare me the sob story. Let's just check the damage. Oh, dear! Are you both still in one piece?"

"Just about – a few scratches, that's all," I lied.

"It's a sin to work on a Sunday," he said, "but tomorrow, I'll get up at the crack of dawn and have your pony all mended by seven. If two of you keep on riding this old nag, mind, it won't last long. What you need is another one – perhaps a smaller filly for you." Our very own old Santa Claus looked at me enigmatically. I stood still, half expecting yet more magic.

"What are you standing there for?" he said. "Let's go and see what we have in the store room."

Miraculously, all my tiredness suddenly evaporated. Old Sid, as he was known in the village, led me to the back of the workshop and took a wooden stepladder off the wall. I quickly took it from him and, showing off my strength, carried it unsteadily around the shed.

"Hey, Hercules! Don't go straining yourself!" the old boy chided. He helped me spread the stepladder and stand it by the back wall. "Now climb up into the loft. There you'll find the parts for a ladies' bicycle. Hand them down to me, one at a time. Only be careful. Don't fall off, or your mother will have me sent to the hard labour camp..."

"What's a hard labour camp?" I asked. The old man smiled. "Better you don't know."

I climbed up to the loft easily, and found all the parts he asked for except for a basket for the back wheel.

"Never mind, I have one somewhere in the scrap heap, from a men's bike, so it's a bit on the large side. Now come down carefully, and bring all the parts into the workshop," he said. After following all his instructions, I wanted to thank my kind mentor.

"Granddad, if you ever need anything urgently from the pharmacy or the shop, just whistle, and I'll be happy to run there and back on your bicycle."

"Right you are, son. I can't whistle anymore but I can always bang my crutch on your gate. Mind you, your ladies' bike won't be ready till tomorrow evening. In the morning, you and your brother will have to ride on the one bike, or take it in turns – whatever you like."

"Honestly, I don't know how to thank you..."

"I've already told you, I don't want your thanks. Beyond those mountains, perhaps somebody is helping my grandchildren as we speak. So we're even. Go and God bless!"

I left feeling overwhelmed by this old man's generosity, and decided to keep the ladies' bike a secret until he had finished assembling it. Let it be a nice surprise for everyone, I thought as I came back home. When Mother asked when the bicycle would be repaired, I told her at seven the next morning. Yosif, however, was worse when the time came. His knee swelled up, and his bruises were black and blue. Mother told me to let the deputy headmistress know that Yosif was ill, and that he would be back at school promptly the following morning. My brother tried to protest but she silenced him, and he went to sulk in his room. When I returned from Old Sid with the repaired bicycle, I found Mother standing in the garden.

"Misha, please take Roman to kindergarten – but push the bike while he's in the saddle. From there, ride to school – and on your way back, please stop at the village shop and pick up everything on this list. Tell them I'll pay as soon as I'm well enough."

I saluted. "Yes, comrade commander, it will be done!" Roman copied me straight away, grabbing his left ear. On my way back from school, I went to the shop. "Auntie," I asked, "you know our neighbour, Old Sidor?"

"Of course. Everyone knows everyone in the village," she replied.

"What sort of thing does he usually buy from you? It's just that we'd like to thank him for his help and kindness."

"What he buys most of is kvass," she said, puzzled, putting a two-litre bottle of the brown liquid on the counter. Noticing my nose wrinkling in distaste, she grew impatient. "Are you buying or not, then? I haven't got all day."

"Yes, yes, I'll take it." I grabbed the heavy bottle with both hands and put it into my half-empty rucksack and handed her the note from Mother.

"Ah, so you're Anna's son. Why didn't you say so, instead of quizzing me about who eats and drinks what," she snapped as she started to put together the items on the list. "What's your name?"

"Misha."

"How old are you?"

"Ten and a half."

"Are you Yosif or the youngest?"

I gave my usual answer. "Neither."

"So what are you, then?" she asked, taking the bait.

"I'm the Golden Middle!" I proudly declared. She smiled.

"And what would that be?"

"You'll find out soon enough, auntie."

"My name is Grusha. I see you're quite a clown."

"Actually, I'm a musician."

"And what do you play, may I ask?"

"The pianoforte."

"The what?"

"The piano," I said, adjusting my language as I finished packing the second bag.

"My regards to your mother. Tell her to get well soon. We'll sort out payment later."

I don't know what our Mother had said to my bruised and battered older brother, but the two invalids had clearly found a lingua franca for half a day. When I cycled home after school, I rang the bicycle bell as usual to signal my arrival. Yosif rushed out to meet me.

"Hello! How's things?"

I didn't miss a beat: "Eight!"

He raised his eyebrows. "What do you mean, 'eight'?"

"What do you mean, 'what do you mean?'"

We both burst out laughing. Yosif took both shopping bags and limped inside with them. I took the bike into the garden, thinking that my brother is either a very good actor, or a chameleon. In the kitchen, I told Mother of Grusha's best wishes and asked if I could give Old Sidor the kvass. She approved of my plan, but said that in future I should ask her permission before, rather than after, buying something. I promised not to make that mistake again.

That evening, I went to see our magician neighbour to pick up the ladies' bicycle. As usual, Old Sid was sitting on the mound. When he saw me coming, he waved and led me into his workshop. There, by the entrance, stood the bike in all its beauty, shiny in a new coat of paint and equipped with bell, light, pump, basket and additional brake. The old man had clearly put his heart and soul into this project, showing off his big heart as well as his extraordinary mechanical talents.

"My son bought this in Kuybyshev for his daughter's birthday, but the war dashed all our plans. He's fighting now, right outside Stalingrad, and his family doesn't come here anymore... There's a padlock and chain in the basket. When you leave it at school, or anywhere else, make sure you lock the back wheel to the frame or to the front wheel. That would be safer. If anyone asks where you got it, tell them I lent it to you just while you're evacuated here."

I drew the bottle from my rucksack. "Grandfather, this is from Mum, as a thank you for all your trouble and kindness."

Recognising the familiar shape, he bowed his head ceremoniously. "Now that's something I won't refuse. Give my deepest respects to your mother. And, Misha, do look after the bike. It's all I have left of my son and granddaughter."

"You have my word as a Musketeer!" I saluted, and rode the bicycle home. Mother and Yosif were waiting for me on the porch, curious to see what I had brought. On seeing the shiny machine, my brother wolf whistled; Mother put her hands to her chest and said, "This is truly a gift from God."

Suddenly remembering, she asked if our benefactor had accepted our modest gift. When I said he sent her his deepest respects, she kissed the top of my head and said, "Well done, son. Now you each have your own transport. I hope you'll truly value this stranger's generosity, and take good care of his gifts."

After dinner, my brother and I had a friendly game of chess. He taught me some new gambits. Roman stood by, observing our game with curiosity, memorising the moves of the pieces as he tried to make sense of it.

Chapter 5

SCHOOL AND PASTIME TUNES

Unfamiliar as it was, our first week at the new school came and went uneventfully. Yosif and I adapted quickly to our new surroundings and soon formed good relationships with our teachers and the other children. We saw each other only on our way to school in the morning and on our way home in the afternoon. Mother started working in the office of the collective farm from eight until noon; they came to collect her and drive her back in a cart pulled by a nag so ancient that the journey was relatively smooth and free of the jolts a more vigorous steed might have subjected her to. Our lives seemed to settle down. Classmates would come round on Sundays and, under Yosif's 'sensitive' guidance, we'd organise a chess training session followed by a tournament. Only boys came, unfortunately, so I had no one to show off to.

Later, Mother discovered an old fishing net in among the junk in the pantry. She repaired the rips and tears, and we stretched it out across the garden between the shed wall and the fence. One of the boys brought a football, and we added volleyball to our games repertoire. A small sign hung by a little chain outside our gate, bearing the inscription: 'The Musketeers Club – free entry, and no guard dog'. Mother gave the guests tea, and they brought honey ginger cake.

All who attended – the mums as well as their offspring – much enjoyed these Sundays. Instead of wasting their time smoking and generally hanging about, the boys were improving their minds with chess and their physical fitness with volleyball. The one shadow hanging over our family life was the absence of any news about Father. Mother had sent our new address to the Central Office long ago, but still no reply came. This may have been because of our frequent moves and change of address; the Centre, inundated by so many similar requests from others, probably couldn't keep up with us. Or so we consoled ourselves.

On the first Sunday in October, Dusya came to say that it was time to dig up the potatoes from the vegetable patch before they got damaged by the impending frosts. She brought a second shovel and showed Yosif and me how to do it. My brother of course grimaced at the sight of the potatoes caked with soil. "I'm not getting my hands all mucky with this dung!" he announced in disgust before riding off on his bike. Taken aback, Dusya just shrugged and returned home, leaving her shovel behind. Mother was upset when she heard what had happened, and looked me in the eyes, reading my thoughts.

"I sympathise, Misha. You've told me more than once that it's unfair to overload one son with all the work. That's why I don't blame you for anything and don't ask anything of you. Go, do what you need to – you have a clear conscience as far as this family is concerned. To coin one of your own expressions: as you make your bed, so you must lie on it."

She turned abruptly and went into the house. I stayed outside on the porch, shovel in hand, not knowing the right thing to do. Should I follow Yosif's dreadful example and go out for a ride on my bike? Or should I stay, hold my tongue and get on with digging out 300 square metres – nearly a hundred plants – on my own? Was Bagheera losing control of her cubs?

I found Mother at the parlour table. She was sitting with her head in her hands, staring at a photograph of father, tears splashing onto the tablecloth. "Why is all this happening to me?" she whimpered. I put my arm around her trembling shoulders and pressed my head against her wet cheek.

"Listen, Mummy, I have a plan," I reassured her. "When Yosif comes back, we'll discuss everything. I'm going to suggest to him that we split the workload. He can dig the potatoes out and I'll clean off the caked soil on the stalks and tubers. All he has to do is stick a shovel into the ground with his foot and keep his little hands clean, and I'll wear thick cloth gloves. Or vice-versa – it's up to him. If he refuses point blank to help, we'll all stand up to him, as a family. In the meantime, let's go and find some sacks and a dark place to store the potatoes, like I saw at Klava's house in Zarnitza."

Mother nodded in agreement, dried her tears with a handkerchief and got up, leaning heavily on my shoulder. In the middle of the hallway, she asked me to roll up the mat and open the door to a cellar, whose existence only she knew about. She lit a candle in a lantern and placed it by the entrance. Cool damp air wafted up from the cellar. Going down on my knees, I noticed a short wooden ladder and some small barrels lined up against the walls. I climbed down and tentatively took the lantern to illuminate my surroundings. There were empty plywood crates and cardboard boxes on shelves, large glass bottles for kvass, huge canvas sacks full to bursting with something or other and some empty jars. All the walls and the floor were coated in cement. The ceiling was covered in wooden panels, with gaps in between for ventilation. Mother sat on the top step, supervising my investigation and explaining what these things were for. I moved around carefully, holding the lantern in my left hand while using my right to feel my way around the contents of the containers, most of which were empty. The sacks turned out to contain rice, wheat, buckwheat and other cereals. Three of them, each weighing some fifty kilogrammes, held bran, the husks separated from wheat after milling. One by one, I handed our commander all the empty crates and enquired about the buckwheat.

She replied matter-of-factly that it could be bought at the village shop with the ration books we received every month, and that we must respect other people's property, no matter what.

After lunch, I went to the vegetable patch before it got dark to count the number of plants and calculate roughly how many kilos there were in every seedbed. When Roman saw the weighing scales, he asked to be enlisted as a helper. He kept lifting the scales up and down with gusto, whether he needed to or not. I counted a total of ninety-six plants, and there were about two kilos of potatoes in the first bed. I estimated that there must be about a hundred and eighty kilos in total. When he heard the final figure, my little brother dropped everything and ran to inform the commander how many potatoes we had to last the winter.

"Don't count your chickens..." came the reply. Roman promptly rushed back to the vegetable patch, where I was down on my knees, digging out potatoes from the second bed. Hearing his approach, I turned to see my little brother sprinting towards me at full tilt, push against my shoulders, and leapfrog over my head.

"You gone loopy, or what?" I shouted.

"Now we're sure to have lots of potatoes for the winter! Mummy said so," he said happily. When I asked her over dinner if this was true, Mother sighed and said, "Just let the child have his innocent little moment of joy."

Yosif didn't return for lunch and was late for dinner, no doubt detained by some chess game or other. Walking past us into the parlour without even turning to look at us he asked, "Anything to eat?"

Mother was darning the holes in our socks. "There are some leftovers in the kitchen," she replied without looking up either. "Heat them up – and mind you wash up after yourself."

Roman and I were playing chess. We exchanged significant glances, anticipating an explosion. While Mother was putting Roman to bed, Yosif was noisily rattling dishes in the kitchen with obvious irritation. "That's just great! Stuffed yourselves and left almost nothing for me!"

Icily, Mother closed the bedroom door and invited us to sit at the round table. My brother knew what this meant: a serious talk. "I have to do my homework for tomorrow," he protested defensively.

"Too bad," Mother said in her steeliest voice. "You should have thought of that earlier." This signalled the futility of any further objection. "As you already know, we're managing to scrape by on the tiny stipend of a serving soldier's family. Nothing else. The collective farm pays me in produce. We have no winter clothes or shoes. As soon as the first frost starts, you'll have nothing to wear to school, or I to work. Our only way out of this situation is to buy the clothes we need from the village shop on account, against the next stipend. That means all of us except Roman will have to go on a compulsory diet. Roman will be fed perfectly well at kindergarten, but we three will have to make do with whatever rations we can get from the village shop, what I get for working at the farm and what we grow on our meagre vegetable patch. It's like the fight for survival in the animal world: those who can't or won't fight pay the price with their lives. Simple as that. As we speak – you can hear it for yourselves on the radio – our country is engaged in a terrible and probably decisive battle against the Nazis, over Stalingrad. For three years now, untold thousands of Soviet soldiers have been selflessly sacrificing their lives, day in and day out, just to keep us safe. Thousands of them, in filthy trenches, enduring hunger, exhaustion, squalor and mortal danger to defend us from possible death. And instead of helping these saviours in their desperate struggle for our nation's survival, some of us are behaving like lily-livered parasites afraid of getting their delicate little hands dirty in the very soil over which our men are spilling their blood!"

This passionate oration gave me goose pimples, and my brother turned red as a lobster. There was no stopping her. "'Not one step back!' our troops are commanded: stop the enemy at any cost. Do you know what that means? That means your father may well be lying dead in a trench, right now, his face buried in this soil my eldest son deigns to call 'mucky dung'!"

She burst into uncontrollable sobs. My brother and I were also crying, our hands over our faces. For all of us, it was as though the emotional floodgates had burst wide open. Later, in our bedroom, before going to sleep, Yosif proposed that we work a couple of hours after lunch all week, in order to have enough time to dig out all the potatoes, clean them, sort them and take them in crates to the cellar – all before the last Sunday in October. I agreed. To avoid any arguments, we decided to split the crop into two equal parts, taking forty or so plants each. That way, we wouldn't have to rely on each other (which is probably why Dusya had brought the second shovel in the first place).

It started getting quite cold at the end of the month, but we managed to get everything done in time. Mother asked each of us to leave one plant for Roman, and on the Saturday he picked every single potato from them, by himself. He spent ages cleaning off every speck of dust with an old toothbrush, tearing off all the white shoots and carefully wiping every potato on his trousers so that he too could bask in his share of our mother's praise. Much later, I understood just how cleverly she was raising her youngest son, to avoid repeating the mistakes she had made with Yosif.

At the beginning of November, when we had acquired our new winter clothes, we Musketeers were in seventh heaven. Once again, circumstances proved Mother right. After these purchases, my brother and I patiently followed the same limited diet every day: porridge in the morning, potatoes, carrots and beetroot for lunch, and milk and biscuits for supper. On the other hand, we had excellent clothes and looked no worse than the other boys at school. Even the teachers noticed.

On November 6th 1942, we celebrated Mother's birthday. At work, she was presented with a large round pie, which the three Musketeers wolfed down with tea. That evening, as she always did on these occasions, our leader made a speech commemorating the anniversary of the famine of the Great October Revolution, after which she told us that the Red Army was preparing a crushing offensive against the enemy, and that victory would soon be ours. Ironically, it was a little earlier that very evening that Hitler announced the defeat of Stalingrad. The familiar tones of the radio announcer Yuri Levitan dismissed this claim as yet more of the Fuhrer's lying propaganda, and urged listeners to disregard the claim as misinformation spread by an enemy intent on sowing panic and disorder. On the contrary, Soviet citizens were urged to renew our war effort and strengthen our victorious spirit for the year ahead.

The last thing we needed at this stressful time was for Mother to fall ill again, but she suffered another prolapse at work through carrying heavy boxes of New Year presents. Distraught, Dusya ran over to tell us that the chairman of the collective farm and his wife had personally taken Mother to the same military hospital as before. Yosif and I were dismayed. We were worried about our mother's health of course, but now the kindergarten and school were closed for the winter holidays. We had also planned trips to Kuybyshev to see the fir tree and the Leningrad circus, and to the mountain camp to learn to ski with our school friends. Everything was going wrong. Instead, we'd have to go to library, stock up on a week's worth of books and just read. Dusya would probably take in Roman again. Poor woman – as if she had nothing else to occupy herself. Still, what else can you do, if you have a big heart and no children of your own?

It was a disastrous turn of events. What about Mother, having us to worry about us while gravely ill herself? And they say there's a God? If there was, He would not have allowed such a cruel fate to befall us, especially not to our mother. I dreaded the tantrums Yosif would start throwing now he was out of our commander's control. Still, no point in expecting the worst before it happens. Time would tell. Dusya's voice interrupted my inner turmoil. She confirmed that she would indeed be picking up Roman from kindergarten that day, and told us to meet her without fail the next day at noon in the parents' room at school. When we asked why, she replied abruptly: "You'll see."

Yosif and I looked at each other with pursed lips. When she asked if we needed any immediate help, we answered, "No, thank you. We know what's what."

"If you need a sledge, there's one in the shed," she added. Somewhat taken aback by the situation, we hadn't even noticed heavy late snowfall outside – a result of the surrounding Zhiguly mountains creating their own microclimate. By morning, a white blanket was spread over the whole village. The smell of freshly baked bread drifted from smoking chimneys. After a rushed breakfast, we decided to clear the snow as best we could with our small shovels, which had probably been made for us by Old Sid. I did the garden while Yosif cleared the street outside our house. Suddenly, my brother called me and pointed at two large wooden snow shovels leaning against the porch. We both smiled, wiping cold snot on our warm sleeves.

"Stupid old idiot!" Yosif exclaimed.

"You grumpy sod!" I said, upset. "After all he's done for us!"

"More fool him. He'd have been better off sitting by the stove, eating his bloody seeds," continued my brother ungratefully. I gave up on him; once a pig, always a pig.

When we'd finished clearing the snow, we put on our new boots and went to school. We kept sinking knee deep in the drifts in the middle of the road, so proceeded at a snail's pace, much to the amusement of the neighbours we knew, who were also busy clearing the snow.

"Hey, Musketeers! Pick your feet up more! This isn't one of your fancy Odessa boulevards!"

At a pre-New Year school parents' committee meeting, the headmistress announced that the Mother of two pupils had just had an accident, leaving them without adult supervision. She asked the mothers present if anyone would be willing to take in one boy, a ten or a twelve-year-old, for the holidays while their mother was in hospital. By then, we were of course already well known to everyone in the school. Moreover, some of the committee members knew us personally, since their sons frequented our Sunday Musketeers' Club. As a result, many people put their hands up. After a brief consultation, we were each allocated to a family, with the proviso that Dusya would supply our food from the village shop and for our fun activities over the New Year, including the trip to Kuybyshev and the ski camp.

Dusya was waiting for us outside school, glad that we had come out at the same time. After taking our boots off in the hallway, we went up to the teachers' room. There, the parents greeted us politely and sympathetically, encouraging us to be strong and prepared in case events took a turn for the worse. The headmistress explained that in these harsh winter conditions, the local authorities did not allow children our age to stay at home by themselves without adult help and supervision. Yosif was about to say something, but she continued regardless: "This is not a matter of personal preference but a statutory requirement. Either you stay with your classmates' families or the local authorities will send you to the nearest orphanage."

On hearing these options, my brother instantly curbed his temper. We were given four hours to get ready and told that our host families would come and pick us up by sledge at six that evening. They gave us a list of necessities and other items we should bring.

"Any questions?" asked the headmistress.

I raised my hand. "We only have one chess set between us. Could we please borrow or buy a second one, so we don't have to fight over it?"

"Don't worry," said the mother in charge, optimistically. "I'll lend you the school gym teacher's own set, tell the village council to give the pupils a special New Year's present, and order ten sets through the village shop. The authorities were asking me only yesterday what an appropriate gift would be for the school. It's an excellent idea. Thank you, boys."

Speak of the devil, I thought, thanking her. My brother sat sulking, like a complete shit. If looks could kill, I would have breathed my last there and then. Feisty Olya, as they called her, was already waiting for us outside, wrapped in a fur coat and holding a whip. Obviously tired of standing still in the freezing cold, the old horse was tossing its tail impatiently, snorting and rhythmically tapping one hoof while nodding its head up and down. Once we'd said goodbye to Dusya, Yosif and I noisily took our places beside our honorary mothers on the big sledge.

Feisty Olya gently urged the horse on, although it needed no encouragement to trot through the deep snow, if only to warm itself up. The women prattled merrily, shouting to one another and at other villagers in the local dialect. As they dropped us off at our house, they reminded us of everything we had to bring for two weeks, told us to lock all the doors and windows and said they'd return for us in four hours' time. Olya bade the horse ride on, leaving deep furrows in the snow and a cloud of flakes in its wake. Yosif and I stood admiring this idyllic winter scene until the convoy disappeared in the distance. It took us two only hours to pack everything on the list into our rucksacks and string bags. I suggested we went to see Sidor. At first, Yosif assumed his usual air of annoyed superiority, but on seeing my determined glare, he conceded.

"You're right, the old boy's going to find it difficult to get around in this snow." We took Sidor's shovels and went to call on him. He was dozing in his favourite spot, dressed warmly, leaning on the crutch that he held firmly in place between his knees. He looked funny, like a neighbourhood Santa Claus. I banged my shovel on the gate.

"Hey! Father Christmas!"

He raised his snow-dusted head. "And who would that be?"

"It's us – the Musketeers from the castle next door!"

"Ah, the bold riders! Then please come in," said Old Sidor, inviting us into the house.

"You just sit there and go back to sleep grandfather, while my brother and I clear some of this snow from your garden. Otherwise, you'll be totally buried in it by morning."

"All right then," he replied, before sinking back into his rabbit fur collar.

We cleared a path from the gate to the porch, and along the wall around the house. Then we supported the old man under the arms and led him to the house. We thanked him for the shovels.

"I made those for you ages ago," he said. "I was just waiting for the right moment to give them to you. God bless, now."

At about six o'clock that evening, as promised, our temporary mothers came to pick us up and take us to their respective homes which, luckily, were in the centre of the village near the library and the shop, halfway between our home and the school. On the way, I made it clear to our guardians on behalf of us both that we had no intention of living with them like parasites, but wanted to share all the household chores, like our classmates, and abide by the same rules as the rest of their family rather than being treated as guests. Yosif could not bear my presumption to speak for both of us, and elbowed me sharply in the ribs. I immediately raised my foot and slammed it across his weak knee. He yelped in pain, but on seeing the women turn to him, he bit his lip and fell silent.

"Don't worry, ladies! We're always horsing around," I reassured them with a smile.

Olya burst out laughing. "I'm beginning to see why Dusya didn't want both Musketeers to be kept together!"

The mothers smiled knowingly, thinking about their own sons. Yosif was the first to be dropped off. He grabbed his heavy rucksack of books and notebooks. His patron took the bulging string bag with his clothes and the chess set, and pointedly wished me a happy stay in my new home. My brother went off sullenly without even saying goodbye. As we continued, I asked my benefactor's name. She said she was Paulina Antonovna, but preferred to be called simply Auntie Paulina. I opened my mouth to introduce myself but she pre-empted me.

"I know almost everything about you, Misha, and I'm sure you'll be happy with us – as long as you don't go kicking my children, like you just did your brother."

I blushed and apologised for the scuffle with Yosif. "Your Andrey and I made friends right at the start of the school year," I told her. "There's no reason why we should fall out. So I can totally guarantee that your children will be safe with me."

As we drove up to my new temporary home, Paulina whispered something into Olya's ear. I almost blurted out that it rude to whisper in front of people but slammed my hand over my mouth just in time.

"Something wrong with your teeth?" asked Antonovna.

"No – just my brain," I joked.

The women exchanged glances. As we said goodbye, Olya put an arm around my shoulders.

"Misha, they say you studied music before the war."

"That's right," I sighed, "the piano."

"My nine-year-old daughter is also learning the piano. Would you like to meet her and play something together?"

"If Auntie Paulina will allow, then – as a Musketeer – I'm always up for anything." The women smiled indulgently.

"Misha, on Monday I'm going to see the headmistress to get the chess set for you and Andrey, but you can go and visit Olya's daughter Zina on Sunday."

"Very well," I said, suddenly sounding like Old Sidor.

"And don't forget, Roman is coming to visit you tomorrow."

Andrey greeted me warmly and took my string bag from his mother. He ushered me straight away into his room, where there was a bed in each corner. One belonged to his three-year-old sister, who was only too happy to be moved to her mother's bedroom. Her wardrobe was emptied for me, and her little table left out for Andrey and I to play chess on. The whole family had made all these changes over a couple of hours, so that I would be comfortable. Quickly putting all my stuff away, I followed Andrey into the garden where there was a large barn divided into sections for different farm animals, including a goat, a cockerel and hens, and two piglets that were to be sold for New Year. There had been three, but one had already been roasted and sent to the Stalingrad front. There were two pairs of skis – one for the father, the other for the son. The father had been killed in action outside Moscow, and ten-year-old Andrey had taken his place as the young master of the house. It was tough for him. He was at school in the morning and, after lunch he had to help his mother around the house. He did his homework in the evening. During the war, all families shared the same aim: to survive in the name of the future generations, in memory of those who had sacrificed their lives to that end.

Paulina called everyone to dinner, and gave me a fresh towel. The Russian soup of suckling pig bones turned out to be so delicious, I practically swallowed my tongue. After such a hearty meal, I relaxed completely. The mistress of the house helped me wash under the freestanding shower, and we all went to bed earlier than I was used to.

At six in the morning, the alarm clock rang under Andrey's pillow. Half asleep, I found myself wondering what on earth Yosif had that would make this unfamiliar ring. On hearing my friend's voice, I soon remembered where I was. In the semi-darkness of his bedroom, he spoke in a whisper and tried to persuade me to go back to sleep. Obstinately, however, I insisted on getting up and mechanically shadowed him wherever he went. Paulina had given me Andrey's spare fur coat and his father's cuffed rubber boots, and I walked out into the garden, yawning. The animals greeted me with a friendly bleating, a chorus of cackles and a duet of squeals. I bowed to them all, and attempted to conduct this morning serenade.

Paulina interrupted my performance and advised me to spend my first day simply observing the show and its protagonists, and not wear myself out by taking on too much before I had any experience of farming. Poor thing

– she had no reason to suspect that I was already well trained in farm work and in conducting Klava's live orchestra, or that I always wanted to show off in front of an audience. Drowsily I carried on, hypnotised, following my young friend, studying all his moves, his relationship with the animals, his technique for feeding and watering them, where their food and the tools were stored. As the sun rose, the imaginary tableaux of my muddled memories of Klava's fairy tale house suddenly disappeared as I adjusted to the harsh reality of my new abode. Fully awake at last, I began to distinguish the goat that Paulina was milking, the two fat and fiercely competitive piglets greedily munching a hearty porridge of husks (as well as each other). The promiscuous cockerel, who serviced about twenty multi-coloured hens, kept leaping aggressively from one to the next, without pausing for a moment's rest.

At breakfast, I wolfed down hot biscuits with what I assumed to be fresh goat's milk, idly reminiscing once again about the start of our evacuation from the Ukraine. Such is life! I decided in future to get all my work things ready the night before, so as not to slow Andrey down first thing in the morning. With a fully functioning helper from the moment we got up, he promised gradually to delegate part of his workload to me so that we'd have more free time later to spend on having fun. I made him promise to teach me to ski before our five-day school trip to the mountains. Although we were the same age, he was much taller and broader than I. He'd have to tighten the straps of the skis and the stick loops to fit me. He promised to do this while I was away on my musical visit to his neighbour, Zina.

Feisty Olya turned out to be the daughter of the collective farm chairman, which accounted for her having her own transport and an expensive musical instrument (by the standards of the time). She took me by the arm from Andrey's gate and led me to her house. On our way, I told her that it had been a whole year since I'd played the piano, and had probably forgotten all the 'accidentals'.

"And what's that when it's at home?" she asked.

"It's a continuous movement of the fingers on the keyboard. I'll definitely need to practise my scales to get the muscle memory back in my hands."

"Well, you'll get the chance to do that with my little daughter. She's a bright and talented girl."

"Just like her mother, then," I remarked, in an attempt to flirt with this beautiful woman.

She grabbed me by the ear. "And you're quite the gallant Musketeer, aren't you?"

"I try, Madam! Only, please give me my ear back!"

The chairman's house looked huge, twice the size of our own little castle. One side was occupied by the old folk, the other by their daughter and granddaughter. On hearing the noise of us fussing around in the hallway, Zina flung open the thickly padded door.

"Welcome!" she said in a resounding voice to her unknown guest, with a bow.

"Good day!" I said, warily. "My name is…"

"Misha-Clown," she pronounced, cutting short my introduction. "And I'm Zina-Ballerina."

I offered my hand formally. She grabbed it and unceremoniously dragged me into the parlour, where the piano stood, its lid already raised. I turned to look at Olya, who stood still with her mouth and eyes wide open in case I was nonplussed by this enthusiastic overture to our musical sessions. Reaching out to her with my free hand, I cried out, "Kind people, I beg you – rescue a poor kidnapped boy!"

We all burst out laughing, defusing any tension. The mother tried to follow us, but her daughter slammed the door shut in her face. I was taken aback by such behaviour, not knowing how to react. Zina sat at the instrument, and started playing the Chopin sonatas laid out before her. The familiar melodies instantly made me nostalgic for my music school and friends in Odessa. The girl played clearly and with a good technique, but without emotion. After finishing another piece, she suggested we played something for four hands. I explained that I had not been near a piano for a long time, and that I needed ten or fifteen minutes to regain some flexibility in my fingers.

"Come on, Clown – don't be shy," Zina snapped, "We're all at your service in this house."

With a sarcastically polite bow and curtsey, she went to her mother in the dining room. I determinedly approached the instrument and carefully started playing scales. My right wrist did well but it was harder to flex the fingers of my left hand after a year of not playing. I fancied I glimpsed Mother's reflection in the polished lid, asking me to play (as she had done) something for my work-weary father. I began with some lyrical Ukrainian tunes and continued with a gypsy rhapsody, so I didn't hear Zina and her mother come into the parlour. Having finished my warm-up, I came back to earth to loud applause from my audience. In response, I took a ceremonial bow and formally conceded my place at the altar of music to its rightful owner.

"Absolutely not!" intervened the mistress of the house. "Now it's time for tea and cakes." Her rebellious daughter was obviously about to protest, but the mother raised her index finger – the 'that's enough' signal in this unusual family. I smiled and promised my new young colleague that, should she be interested, we could continue having our piano meetings. At the table, Olya asked me about father and our evacuation. I answered half-heartedly, trying to change the subject to the forthcoming New Year celebrations. Zina went to the same school as us, a class below me, and took an active part in all artistic activities. She sang, danced and played in the folk orchestra. In other words, she was the local star.

I told Olya that Dusya and my youngest brother were supposed to visit me at Paulina's house after lunch. Thanking the lady of the house for her hospitality, I told her not to worry because I'd find my own way back to my new home. Even so, she gave me detailed directions. Zina promised that next time I visited she would teach me to dance, as she needed a partner for the school ensemble. I replied that she'd have more success with an elephant or a hippo, but Olya insisted that her daughter could even teach a stool to dance.

Dusya and Roman were already waiting for me at Paulina's. While the women talked business, I took my little brother into the garden to introduce him to the animals. He gingerly stroked the goat but could not bring himself to trust the shrill piglets that were begging to be patted. Most of all, he was interested in the hens that were half asleep on the racks, inside straw baskets to catch the eggs, and in the proud, multi-coloured cockerel who stood on high alert. When Roman, without thinking, tried to stroke the nearest hen, the head of the family spread his abundant tail in a fan and, with a shrill squawk, tried to peck my little brother's outstretched hand. I quickly clicked my fingers in front of the attacker's beak to divert his attack in my direction. Like a general in full regalia, the bird walked over the bar and turned his splayed tail to us. In the bat of an eye, I pulled the frightened Roman down towards me, and we crouched down. At that very moment, the handsome cockerel squirted a jet of emerald green guano with impressive accuracy at his unwanted houseguests. The little one stared at me in surprise.

"How did you know the cockerel was going to p-p-poo at us?"

"I saw the same thing happen at Klava's house, in Zarnitza."

"Is that where you kept falling off the horse?"

"Yes, comrade-Sir. The very place."

Roman loved to be addressed in a military manner. When I asked if he'd already seen Yosif, he replied that Auntie Dusya had taken him by sledge to see Yosif first, and that they'd played two games of chess. Then she had brought him back for lunch, which I'd missed because I was late.

"Art demands sacrifice," I confessed sadly, looking at the little one. For some reason, I suddenly felt sorry for him. Why did he have to go through all these ordeals?

"What are you staring at me like that for?" he asked, puzzled.

"I just want to take you for a ride on the sledge. You're not scared, are you?"

"It's all right if I'm with you," he conceded.

I asked Dusya where the nearest suitable slope was. "We'll go for a ride while you two talk."

Andrey immediately latched onto the idea and said there was a good mound for sliding down nearby, and that he'd come with us the first time, as insurance against the local competitors.

"No more than an hour," Dusya instructed, 'And don't leave the little one on his own!"

She made sure Roman was well wrapped up from top to toe, and we dashed out of the house with two sledges – Dusya's small one, and Andrey's larger one. My little brother and I followed obediently in their footsteps. With his long legs, Andrey dragged Roman on the sledge so fast that even though mine was empty, I could barely keep up. Laughing in delight, Roman kept yelling, "Hey! Misha! Keep up! Come on, pick your feet up!"

I didn't mind. On the contrary, it was lovely to see him so happy. I kept tripping over deliberately, tumbling into the piled snow and leaping back up again to catch up with my giggling little brother. Sitting backwards on the sledge, he kept stretching out a helping hand, but I could never quite reach it, repeatedly falling on my face in front of him. Finally, we reached the stables of the collective farm, behind which there was a hilly clearing on which animals grazed in the summer. Now, though, you could hear the boisterous cries of children, just like at the Privoz flea market in Odessa.

Although Roman was a little anxious the first time we slid down, the subsequent ascents and dizzying downhill slaloms gave him, as we say in Odessa, a world of joy. He shrieked and laughed more than anyone else, totally surrendering himself to the unadulterated pleasures of childhood. We didn't even notice time pass; Andrey had to remind us that we'd promised to be back in an hour, so we rushed home. Understandably, the little one did not want to leave such a fun place, but complied once we warned him that Dusya would tell us off. On the way back, he was so tired that he fell asleep on the sledge, his face glowing and a happy smile on his lips. Andrey and I also smiled, pleased with ourselves at the sight of my little brother so contented.

Spotting us from the window, Dusya ran out into the cold in what she was wearing, afraid that something had happened to Roman. But as soon as she saw the sleeping cherub, she forgot to scold us for being late and took the sleepy little one into the house. Andrey and I went to check on his animals. Roman ran to thank Andrey before leaving, as Dusya had taught him to, and went to shake his hand – but when he saw his gloves encrusted with chicken shit, shied away in disgust, and decided to say goodbye to the goat instead. Taken by surprise, the beast struck a defensive pose. It lowered its head and pointed its horns towards the unwelcome intrusion. My little brother stepped back with a frightened shriek, which so startled the goat that it reared up on its hind legs and began kicking its front hooves to ward off its potential assailant, small as he was. Sheer terror made Roman fill his trousers less than fragrantly, and his wails rang out across the village. Andrey immediately interposed himself between the protagonists, reassuring the agitated goat that all was well. Duly calmed, the animal returned to its corner, but its unwitting little aggressor continued to tremble in shock for a long time in Dusya's arms.

Every other day, Mother's colleagues from the village council and the collective farm visited her at the military hospital and gave her news of us. This time, the doctors decided to keep her in for an extra week to ensure a better outcome from the operation. Constantly worrying about us, she often wept. When the ward supervisor allowed her to speak with us for three minutes on his radiotelephone, Dusya brought us into the chairman's reception room, where we waited in some trepidation for the call. When the old apparatus finally rang, Dusya grabbed the receiver and hastily whispered some important news to Mother before giving it to my brother, while glancing constantly at the wall clock. After a series of monosyllabic questions and answers, he passed the receiver to me. Instead of listening to Mother, I recited the report I had prepared and reassured her when she asked how Yosif and I were getting along. I handed the receiver to Roman, who promptly started to cry and whined for her to came back home.

"Annushka, don't worry – everything will be all right,' the secretary shouted into the mouthpiece over the little one's sobs. "Just get well!"

As she took us back to our homes, Dusya became quite upset herself, unable to console my little brother, who kept whimpering, "I want my Mummy…"

Yosif and I looked at Roman dejectedly, aware that there was nothing we could do to help. Never mind, I kept repeating to myself, this isn't the end. Before we left, father had urged us never to lose courage, no matter how hard things were. Even if one of us faltered, even if the situation seemed hopeless, we had to look for a solution, attempt the impossible, find a compromise, but never, ever give up.

Dear father, I reflected, that all sounds fine in theory, but when it comes down to it, real life is a different matter. You told us always to stick together and never let go of one another. But even though we did try to stay together, circumstances have snatched our mother away from us and separated us from each other against our will. Why? Life isn't as easy as that. Things aren't black or white, true or false. Don't you agree?

We spent an entire day getting ready for our trip to Kuybyshev to see the fir tree. Our honorary mums laundered, ironed and darned our modest clothes as well as their children's and trimmed our hair and nails so as to usher in the New Year 1943 smartly, and to mark the start of our victory over the Nazi hordes. In the morning, two old buses from the Zhiguly depot drove fifty or so pupils and their teachers into town to see the New Year circus show. Certain main roads were regularly cleared of snow, so it took us only a quarter of an hour to reach the Volga, and as long again to cross the frozen river. There were no trained animals in the circus, but it was fun nonetheless. Clowns played their scenes of comic animosity, and there were trapeze artists, musical acts, wire dancers, acrobats and groups of jugglers. In the finale, a large decorated fir tree rose up from the floor in the centre of the arena, which both the performers and the audience danced around.

At the beginning of January, after two days of preparation, we finally went to the winter sports camp for five days, escorted only by the gym teacher and the senior leader. The small Finnish huts could accommodate four people, and were heated with pot-bellied paraffin stoves; the toilets were outside so, in case of necessity, speed was of the essence to avoid freezing the more delicate parts of one's anatomy. We slept on the floor in the corners of the room, on thick woollen mattresses. Tea was boiled on the stove, and we drank it with cold sandwiches. We all found these primitive comforts rather romantic.

We were impatient for the ski training and sledging to begin. Understandably, I ended up in the beginners group; Andrey was in the intermediates and to my surprise, my musical partner in crime Zina was in the advanced group. Andrey answered my questioning glance: "She's an ace at skiing, the school champion. You'll soon see why if you watch her technique and style."

"So she's a star here too, is she?" I said, rather dismissing her talents.

"Hey, brother, you'd better hold your tongue or – excuse me – shove it where the sun don't shine."

At seven, we were woken by the gym teacher's whistle and the group leader. We had a thirty-minute outdoor workout of special exercises, and thirty minutes to eat breakfast, wash and put on all our winter sports clothes ready to start our training session (in separate groups for boys and girls) at eight o'clock.

I enjoyed watching Zina's skill on the slopes. Olya's daughter was indeed by far the best of her group. I wasn't surprised. Admittedly, she had the natural gift of physical grace, performing talent and rhythm – but unlike other talented children, Zina-Ballerina also had the means to pay for private training sessions with the group leader. Her mother also instilled a Spartan attitude in her daughter, and even in those tough times, was able to give her everything she needed to develop her academic, sporting and artistic talents. Zina's graceful movements, emotional confidence, unwavering focus and uncommon willpower made her stand out from the rest in the training session like a bright star, even though she was still young and not very tall. I suddenly felt something move me inside. Misha, your tongue's hanging out, I told myself – as if you've never seen a brighter star. Don't be so daft, you bow-legged Musketeer! Go on, admit it, you're just jealous of someone else's success.

The leader's whistle signalled time for bed. For a long time, the shapes of skiers flashed before my eyes. After five days of intensive training in the fresh air and idyllic surroundings, we all grew so close that we felt as though we'd always lived in this enormous happy family. We simply hadn't had the time to miss our real families and friends. The same two rickety buses from the village centre drove us back to Vypolzovo; we were so excited that the driver kept having to beep his horn to make us calm down. Smiling mothers met us at the municipal building, happy to see their children back safe and sound after a good sporting holiday.

I was met by Yosif, no doubt on Dusya's instructions. Picking up my skis, he said Mother was feeling much better and that, all being well, they would discharge her from the hospital the following Sunday. Yosif, Dusya and I spent all the next day cleaning and heating the house, and preparing fresh food to give our mother the best possible welcome.

Sunday came, but she did not arrive. The head of the hospital had ordered another week of bed rest, constantly attended by a nurse. The village council chairman called his secretary and the headmistress as a matter of urgency. After an animated discussion, they decided that the secretary would release Dusya from work for a week so that she could take care of Anna while looking after us. The school nurse would also visit the patient every day after work for a week. The host mothers were heartily thanked for their help in taking in parentless children.

On Monday, Olya drove us home after school with our belongings. There, we found Mother attended by Dusya and the nurse; not having seen us for two whole weeks, she became very emotional. We thanked Olya and kissed her on the cheek, and Mother gave her a grateful nod. Olya managed to whisper in my ear that Zina very much wanted to see me again. I promised her I'd arrange another meeting when I next saw her at school, before rushing into Mother's bedroom. Yosif was already there, giving her a full report on how he had been to the circus but not to the winter sports camp as he preferred to stay in the library and to play chess.

As a New Year's present, the school received twenty chess sets from the two council and collective farm chairmen. The headmistress had suggested that from the next term onwards, Yosif should organise a voluntary chess club in the library every Saturday afternoon from two until six, under the supervision of the parents' committee. Mother was also pleased to hear that her eldest had completed his first term with top marks in every subject. To my delight, the deputy head decided to move me up to the fourth form, since I already knew the syllabus of the third and kept bothering the other pupils by prompting their answers.

The hospital sent through Mum's medical notes. The two operations had left her with complications which, according to the doctor, entitled her to a disability allowance. Dusya got all the relevant documents ready and gave them to Olya, so that she could apply to Social Services for Mother's allowance the next time she went to Kuybyshev on business. That way, our mother would have a supplementary income and would no longer have to work as before and, as Dusya said, run herself into an early grave. When Olya returned from town, she said that it would take at least a month for Social Services to reach a decision; for the time being, we would have to be patient. But our patience was in short supply. Mother's remuneration in food stopped arriving from the collective farm. Except for potatoes, our stock of groceries ran out. Our food rations were cut because of the dire need to supply the army. The only way out of this crisis was to sell any surplus of potatoes on the market, just as our neighbours did.

During the school break, I saw Zina and complimented her on the excellence of her skiing. As usual, she curtseyed to acknowledge the compliment and asked if I would like to be her partner in the school dance ensemble.

"Are you sure that won't harm your reputation?" I asked.

"Oh, enough with the ifs and buts! Is that a yes or a no?"

"Of course it's a yes! How could I possibly decline such an honour? When?"

"Tuesdays and Friday, two till four."

"That's tomorrow!"

"Yeah!" she said casually, before running off.

What's the rush? I said to myself and in my distraction, ran to the third form as before. Suddenly realising my mistake, I abruptly changed direction, nearly knocking the teacher off her feet in the process. Even at that tender age, the fair sex can drive a fellow crazy…

The new young teacher made me feel surprisingly welcome, considering that circumstances had led me to join her class in the second half of the year. The deputy head had obviously briefed her about this delicate transition. Within an hour, she had shown me what I had missed, replaced my third form books with fourth form ones and given me two weeks to catch up. I sat mugging up on every subject until ten o'clock every night, when Mother came to send me to bed. My determination to keep up with my new classmates and not embarrass the deputy head who had recommended me to the new teacher, yielded a small miracle. By late January, I was almost on a par with everyone else in my class. The teacher was pleased with me. I was not a total stranger to the boys, since many already knew me from the Musketeers' Club and the winter sports camp. In short, I managed to integrate into the fourth form much quicker that I had thought.

The next morning, Zina came looking for me in the third form, where Andrey told her I had moved up to the fourth. Thinking he was joking, she asked, "Why not the fifth?"

"Misha will tell you that himself," Andrey smiled. Catching me at the entrance to the fourth form, she whispered in my ear: "Don't forget, two o'clock, sports hall."

I nodded and followed her with my eyes. My classmates were nosey.

"What was she whispering?"

"She was just telling me to meet her in the sports hall... after lunch," I joked, in a daze.

They laughed. "Be careful, Musketeer! Your sword won't protect you from her!"

"You can't run away from fate," I replied. Still, I knew I was definitely trapped.

"How could you let yourself be caught so easily? You, you never lose, and now she's got you right around her little finger!"

"That's no little finger – that's a sharp little claw."

Speak of the devil. Little Zina had obviously worked out that I was not made of wood, and that I would come running for any opportunity to perform. Moreover, like any woman, she had seen that I liked her, and taken advantage. That's how men, no matter how young or old, lose their freedom and independence under the spell of so-called love.

As soon as I was invited to partner Zina, I knew that the dance instructors would want to assess my abilities. I knew full well that, after two years of life as an evacuee, my performance skills, muscle memory and artistic confidence were shot to ribbons. So I tried to access what was left in my mental and physical memory of the gypsy dances I had known. I practised in the corner of the sports hall after class and, in the evening, in our parlour at home. Our mother came in when she heard the floorboards creak.

"What is it, son? Are you getting ready to go the ballet school?"

"Not yet, Mummy. It's just for the school ensemble."

"All right. Just make sure you don't crack your head open."

I suddenly remembered the enchantress in Odessa – the old gypsy next door. She often sang and played the guitar while her grandson danced. I would immediately catch on to his movements and, like a monkey, copy the graceful nuances of his gypsy dance. The old woman had often said that I had a brilliant career as a dancer ahead of me.

When the instructors asked me what I had ever danced, I replied, "The Ukrainian Gopak, the Russian folk dance, the sailor dance, the Moldavian and the gypsy dance."

"Show us," they said. I had practised a little the night before, and was waiting for an opportunity to show off in front of my new partner.

"I'll try and remember what I can, if you could play for me *The Two Guitars* from the gypsy repertoire. *Andante* to start with, then speeding up to *allegro vivace.*" The accordionist picked up his instrument, and I sang him the opening bars of the familiar melody. While he tried to remember the variations, I crouched a few times, shook my limbs, stretched my body and turned my head round and round, like a professional. Long ago, in peacetime, I had watched the rehearsals of the Ukrainian Folk Ensemble, and the dancers' preparatory warm-up stayed in my memory. Zina watched, her eyes on stalks, and the domra player smiled knowingly. The accordionist checked the accelerating tempo and the variations with me, and I confirmed that I was ready.

To be honest, I was a little nervous after not doing anything since the start of the war. Still, in for a penny, in for a pound. I assumed the starting position. After a musical introduction, I began to promenade, slapping my thighs, then progressed to a comic scissor leg movement with a trick knee spring. I gradually went into a trance and forgot my audience. The musician played with passion, and took me to the heights of gypsy ardour. I pictured myself at an Odessa party where all the guests were transported by my dancing, along with the accompanist. I suddenly heard the lifeless room break into enthusiastic cries and whistles. I began tap dancing to the rhythm of the clapping, and squatting to the beat of the drum, transported into an ecstatic state. It was as though I had become someone else.

Against all the reality around me, I longed to prove to them all that I had survived the atrocities of war and not lost any of the artistic fire in my spirit; that our mother had survived and was still with us; that hunger and cold had no hold over us – not now, not ever – as long as we held onto one another. It was the scream of a soul in torment, who nonetheless had an unshakeable faith in a brighter future. Where did I find the energy and breath to keep up this two-minute improvisation, lacking as I was in regular training? It must have come from somewhere bigger and stronger than me. In the end, I leapt up only to drop down on my knees before the instructors, arching my back and expecting applause.

None came. The girls stood silent, waiting for the teachers' reaction, as the latter discussed my performance. Sweat – and uncontrollable tears – dripped from my face onto the linoleum floor. Zina rushed to me with a towel, and helped me to my feet.

"Look at you, Misha! Where do you learn all that?"

"Gypsy friends back in Odessa," I stammered, still breathless from the exertion. "I'm so unfit after two years of war."

"Never mind. I'll help you the first few times, and I promise I won't split hairs."

"You're not what worries me, Zina. It's just that it's a bit awkward for me to be the only boy here, with all the girls. You must understand that."

Our conversation was interrupted by the instructors. I thanked the accordionist for playing. The domra player asked if I would like to dance with their group where, unfortunately, there were only girls. I felt uneasy, not expecting this.

"I was invited here by Zina, on your behalf, to be her partner. I'll do whatever you think best. I'm just a bit discouraged that there are no boys here except for me. If you put up an advertisement, I'll try and persuade my friends to come and try it out."

The musicians exchanged knowing looks. "Misha, you have a talent for stage performance and a good sense of rhythm." I gave a grateful nod. "We can devise something special for you and Zina. Would you be interested or do you want something more?"

"In my limited experience of dancing at school, I think that if I'm here on my own, the boys will constantly be pestering me with taunts, if only out of jealousy. That's for sure. I think it's definitely worth trying to involve other people interested in dancing – not just by advertising but also through the parents' committee. Zina and I can rehearse a simple Moldavian suite or a Kazachok in our own time and, once you've corrected us, we can give a demonstration to the boys. Their mothers will encourage them, and so will we. I can also show them some nice movements of the Sailor's Dance, like tapping, clapping, crouching and so on. I'm sure that if we use me as bait, we could land a really big fish here. In any case, if you never try, you never get."

The domra player asked if I could play the dances I mentioned on the piano, so that they could be written down to accompany the demonstration and any future performances. I promised to go home and try and remember the folk tunes for every dance. Then, with Zina's help, we could transcribe the score. Although the instructors looked interested in the potential of the group, something seemed to worry them. It was either the pressure put on by Zina and her mother, or my exaggerated enthusiasm about the boys, or perhaps the temporary nature of my family's stay in Vypolzovo – I didn't know. There was something they weren't saying. In any case, Zina agreed to get together every Saturday after her chess session from two till four to practise the Moldavian dance and the Kazachok, which, having danced it many times before, I could choreograph by myself, including the woman's steps. Zina was very happy. My chances as a Musketeer increased by the day. Even Olya, when she came to pick up her daughter, gave me a kiss on the forehead on hearing the good news.

Chapter 6

TRIALS OF BODY AND SOUL

Little by little, Mother regained the strength to take over running the household from Dusya. Yosif made sure he brought us food from the village shop and from our cellar, while I took care of sweeping the snow from the garden and outside our house. We took it in turns to bring in the firewood and light the stove. We tried to get everything done by six o'clock so that we could do our homework after dinner. Mother supervised our regime strictly and helped me to catch up with the fourth form work.

In March though, our financial situation took a dramatic turn for the worse. We couldn't bear to look at a potato any more, let alone eat them; although we had food rations, there was no produce to spend them on in the village shop. All the country's reserves went to supply the advancing army. There was no one to complain to, nor any point in doing so.

Every Wednesday and Saturday at six a.m., the women in our neighbourhood would carry buckets full of potatoes on yokes to Kuybyshev market – a twelve-kilometre journey, plus a steam ferry ride across the Volga. They arrived at the market at ten and traded until two, after which they bought their own provisions in town with the money they had made, returning exhausted to their homes and families at eight p.m.

At Dusya's instigation, our nearest neighbours agreed to take me or my brother with them to market once a week and to watch over us to make sure that we weren't cheated by customers or robbed by pickpockets. Yosif wouldn't hear of such a thing, preferring to starve to death. It was clear to me that I'd have to take this task upon myself. There was no point in getting bitter about it or trying to persuade my parasitic older brother; I just had to keep the promise I had made to our father. Dusya explained the situation to the deputy headmistress, and they decided that Wednesday would be the most convenient day to miss classes, and the least dangerous day at the market as far as thieves and roughnecks were concerned. I didn't know how to use a yoke, and my shoulders were probably too small, so my bucketful of potatoes was divided into two parts in a half-empty bag, which was then tied with a string in the middle and slung across one of my shoulders. That way, I could swap shoulders at any time as I walked. In the gloom of the evening, I practised carrying this weight along the local streets.

One bucketful of potatoes bought only one loaf of bread, but we could also redeem our ration tokens in any of the town's grocery shops, as long as I was accompanied by an adult to vouch for me and confirm that the tokens weren't stolen. Mother compiled a list of the bare essentials and household items I had to buy from private sellers, or exchange for ration tokens in the shop. Mother worried about sending me out on this adventure.

"Misha, if you feel you're not up to this, stay here at home." Her hands trembled on my shoulders. "We'll find a way to manage, somehow."

"Mummy, don't worry. Give me at least one chance. I promise I'll be careful and come back safe and sound. I give you my word as a Musketeer!"

Smiling, she pressed my head against her bosom and whispered, "Thank you, son. Your father would be proud of you." Our Bagheera evidently felt a twinge of maternal guilt at her cub's first sortie alone into the wide world.

On the Tuesday night, I prepared the bag with the potatoes. Mother gave me a shopping list, her medical prescriptions and a special purse on a ribbon, which I was to wear under my shirt at all times. I went to bed straight after dinner; at five the next morning, the smell of barley porridge wafted up from the kitchen. I warbled 'Rise, you marked soul' to myself as I stood over the piss bucket. Once I'd washed, I went into the kitchen, where a bowl of steaming porridge and some unsweetened tea stood waiting for me on the table. I felt as though I was being sent on a reconnaissance mission or a military operation – a ploy which helped to disguise my anxieties about the task ahead.

By six, I was armed and ready. A tap on the window announced the arrival of the women neighbours. Mother slipped a flask of water and a wedge of bread into my coat pockets and hugged me.

"God bless, son!"

I stood up straight. "Yes, comrade Commander!" I tossed the bag lightly over my shoulder and went to join my travelling companions.

"Good morning, Aunties!" I said confidently from the porch.

"Good morning, Uncle!" replied the eldest. She greeted my mother, who was standing at the door. "How old is he?" she asked.

"Ten," Mother smiled.

"And a half," I corrected her.

"Well, then – if you're ten and a half, that's all right then! My name's Anna. I have two boys like you of my own."

"And I'm Fedora. These are my daughters and my daughter-in-law. Our house is at the end of the street, on the left. Dusya told us about you. We'll be happy to help you out, as long as this uncle here promises not to do anything without my permission until we get back home. Have you got money for the ferry?" I nodded. "A purse for your money?" I touched my neck. "Water and bread?" I slapped my pockets. "Head on your shoulders?" I swayed my head uncertainly, and pursed my lips. Everybody burst out laughing.

"Anna, expect us back at sunset."

All four women then simultaneously lifted up their yokes onto their shoulders and, balancing buckets overloaded with vegetables, started to walk. The narrow strip of light on the horizon was growing noticeably wider. As we left the village, the noisy chorus of cockerels and goats, punctuated by the occasional bark, gradually faded out of earshot. The sky was clear, and the stars paled above our heads. The road, damp with dew, snaked between the Zhiguly Mountains. The silence was broken only by the sound of our heavy footsteps. The women didn't speak, to preserve the rhythm of their breathing for the journey ahead. I followed their example, and took deeper and more even breaths: three paces, breathe in; three more paces, breathe out. I had trouble synchronising my breathing with counting my steps at first, but after a while, I found my own rhythm and began studying the springtime mountain landscape around me. Although the peaks were still covered in snow, fresh green stems were already sprouting out of the cold damp earth in the valleys, and buds swelled in the bushes by the roadside. After about an hour, Fedora announced that it was time for a break.

"Are you tired, little man?" she asked, sympathetically.

"A little, but it's not too bad so far," I lied. Even though I often moved my bag from one shoulder to the other, my neck vertebrae started to feel painful after a while. I carefully put my bag down on a flat rock and sighed with relief. After doing some exercises to relax the muscles of my neck, shoulders and body, I sat down on the rock. Seeing that the women were drinking water, I took out my flask and put it to my lips. Although I wasn't thirsty, I tried to copy the behaviour of these experienced walkers without waiting for them to tell me. The women exchanged knowing glances, obviously approving of my intention to benefit from their experience.

"Son, if you get to the point where you just can't manage it, just this first time, we'll each take ten potatoes off you – half your load – and give them back to you on the way."

"Thank you, Auntie Fedora. I've had a rest and relaxed my muscles. I hope I can reach our destination without your help. After the trading though, I'll need an adult to come with me to claim the food rations in a grocery store."

"Yes, I know. Dusya has already told me. That won't be a problem, because we need to buy things too, so we can all do it together. And now, Musketeers and wenches – back in the saddle!"

I asked to 'get some air'. While the women were getting ready, I dashed behind the rock for privacy and, after shedding some personal weight, felt fitter as well as 200g lighter.

We walked the rest of the way beneath the rays of the rising sun, which soon disappeared behind the peaks. My shoulders started to ache again, and I felt muscle spasms in my calves. I longed to stop and massage them, but did not give in. I tried to breathe more deeply and to lean my hands on my hips, but it was no good. As I shifted the load from one shoulder to the other, I accidentally rested it behind my head, evenly distributing the load between my shoulders. The pain immediately subsided and, happy with my discovery, I began to walk more confidently with the cross I had to bear. Oh, how I sympathised with Jesus at that moment, carrying his holy load till he lost his strength, neither complaining nor asking for help. In the village library, Yosif had once showed me a book called *The Utopia of Religion*, with pictures of various deities. Despite being forbidden to children, my brother secretly showed me icons of the Madonna and Child, of George the Saviour, of the crucified Christ and so on. Our parents considered themselves non-religious, but why in that case had Mother said "God bless, son," to me when she said goodbye to me that morning? I couldn't understand it. Adults must get things even more mixed up than their children, I concluded. Preoccupied with such insoluble dilemmas, I didn't even notice we had reached the pier.

"Misha, get three roubles ready to give to the ferryman." The adult fare was five roubles; a kilo of potatoes cost between ten and fifteen roubles, depending on quality. I asked one of my companions to help me take the bag off my shoulders, as I felt a sudden pain in my lower back. She put the bag down next to me and paid me a compliment. "Good on you, boy, you carried your own load yourself."

"Just doing my best, Comrade," I said, trying to give myself courage, holding my lower back. Everyone laughed, mistaking my gesture for a joke. I played along. "The most important thing is to keep up appearances."

When Fedora returned with the tickets, I asked her, "Where's mine?"

"You have to go and pay yourself – there are no children's fares."

I stared back, not understanding what I was supposed to do. Fedora felt sorry for me. "Oh, poor little uncle lost his head somewhere back in the mountains."

She carefully took the three roubles from my hand and gave them to the ferryman. He threw them in his bag without looking, and sounded the whistle to depart. Fedora had no idea how right she was about my inner state. I'd managed to last the walk to the ferry, driven by my initial enthusiasm, but my body was now paying the price. Steadying myself on the railing, I looked down over the water but could see nothing but darkness. I dimly heard muffled voices of people and snorting horses. I had just one thought: not to fall into the murky waters below. Obviously noticing the state I was really in, Fedora stood by, ready. She splashed water from her flask onto my face and wiped it dry with her scarf. She sat me on the bench, and gently slapping my cheeks to make me come to. I opened my eyes and saw four kind eyes staring worriedly back. "What happened?" I whispered, confused.

"Everything's all right, brave Musketeer. You managed to find your head and put it back on your shoulders. Now just you make sure you hold onto it!"

192

"I'll hold onto it," I muttered faintly, raising my head, straightening my back and dropping my shoulders. The stares turned into smiles, and I was rewarded with a dry prune. The cool river breeze quickly restored me to my senses. I started playing with the horses and joking with my companions as if nothing had happened. When we reached the far bank, Fedora renewed her offer to relieve me of part of my load. I thanked her, saying, "I don't need it yet. I want to try and complete my mission myself. But if I can't, I'll put my hands up."

She wished me luck: "God help you, then." I saluted, and they loaded the half-ton bag (well, at least eight kilos) onto my shoulders. We walked slowly onto the shore. At about ten, we arrived at the market which, fortunately, was close to the pier. There were many vacant stalls, and we installed ourselves in five of them, all in a row, right by the entrance. I was placed in the middle, where my protectors could easily keep an eye on their protégé. Fedora kept making suggestions on how to make the goods look better, how to attract customers, how to make bundles of potatoes wrapped in newspaper bags, and how to count the money.

Having thanked my neighbours, I managed to sell my potatoes in about two hours. The rest of the time, I helped them weigh out their vegetables on scales and pack them in newspaper bags. Once we finished trading, we counted our earnings, packed up, and went to the nearest tearoom for a well-earned snack. Fedora took my shopping list and Mother's prescriptions so as to plan our shopping expedition. She sorted everything into different types of product and advised me not to buy anything on my own in case the vendors tried to pull the wool over my eyes.

"What do you mean?" I asked, not understanding.

"It means they'll swindle you," said the daughters, laughing.

I stared back. "Oh, I see. The penny's dropped."

"You have the neck of giraffe – by the time something reaches your head, your feet have got cold."

I joined in the young women's convivial laughter, but had no idea what they meant. "What have cold feet got to do with anything?"

This time, Fedora replied in her deep voice. "When animals die, the first thing that happens is that their feet go cold. Got it now?" I decided to keep my stupid mouth shut.

We began our shopping at the pharmacy. Fedora produced Mother's prescriptions, and the old pharmacist quickly put together the necessary medicines, for which I duly paid.

The grocery store proved more problematic because the assistant refused to accept my ration tokens for the previous two months on the grounds that they were out of date. Fedora calmly explained that there had been no produce at our village shop for three months, but the vendor insisted that the tokens were no longer valid. Fedora promptly demanded to see the manageress. The long queue began protesting at the delay. At this point, the three younger members of our party came to the rescue by interposing themselves between the queue and the counter. "Citizens, don't worry. Don't give in, because tomorrow, these creatures may well decide to deny you groceries, too. Is this what our husbands are fighting and dying at the front for? We must stick together and not let petty bureaucrats take us for a ride!"

When the manageress appeared and demanded quiet and order, Fedora grabbed me by the scruff of the neck like a puppy. "This child's father is on the front," she declared fiercely. "His mother is gravely ill. There are two more children like him at home. They've had no bread or salt for three months because of the District Food Distribution Office's useless organisation. The local authorities have said that evacuated families can only redeem their tokens here. This child has just walked twelve kilometres, and you stand there telling him that he should eat these tokens instead of bread?"

It was like throwing a match into a barrel of gunpowder. The three young women were waving their fists. "Monsters! You should all be stood up against the wall!"

Tempers flared among the people in the queue. "Villains! Animals! Crooks!"

In the face of such an angry mob, the trembling assistant turned white with fear. The manageress took the stack of unused tokens from Fedora, together with Mother's shopping list, and curtly instructed her to wait for ten minutes before disappearing behind the shelves.

Although the customers gradually calmed down, they continued talking about embezzlement, speculation and the general mayhem for some time. Fedora took me by the hand and led me into a corner, saying, "Just stay here and don't interfere."

While she and her daughters went off to different stores to do their own shopping, I sat on the floor in the corner, my arms around my knees, studying the locals. City people seemed harder and more demanding than village folk, I thought. No one paid any attention to me, as though I wasn't there. They must have been so used to seeing homeless beggars in the streets here that they simply ignored them, even though some may have not eaten or slept for a long time, or might need medicine or a mother's love...

The manageress's voice distracted me from my sad thoughts. She asked for my empty bag and returned Mother's shopping list, without the tokens. A minute later, she returned from behind the counter with my bag, half full and tightly secured with string. Fedora suddenly appeared from nowhere; she must have been keeping an eye on me all the time. The manageress turned to her.

"We've done everything we could for this family," she nodded in my direction. "Next time, the child must come with an adult at the beginning of the month. It'll be much easier then to redeem the tokens. If he asks for me, we can sort everything out without having to stand in a queue."

My mission commander Fedora and I thanked her in unison, and prepared to continue with our shopping elsewhere. As we came out of the grocery store, Fedora confided: "Sorry about that, son, but the girls and I had to raise a bit of hell in there."

"I understand completely," I nodded." You had to give as good as you got."

In the household goods store, I had to pay in cash, of which I had precious little. All the haberdashery and toiletry items on Mother's shopping list cost more than my limited funds allowed. Fedora immediately grasped the situation and offered to lend the money for our modest needs. I took it upon myself to accept, knowing full well that our mother would not be happy about such an arrangement. Might as well be hanged for a sheep as a lamb, I thought, as I struggled to untie the double knot the grocery store manageress had made on my bag, and put in the final items. I was curious to see what was wrapped in the food bags and in the packets, but there was no time to investigate now. Laden with shopping, we went to the pier to catch the five o'clock ferry. Although very tired, I was buoyed by the immense satisfaction of having accomplished my mission. We rested on the ferry for half an hour, watching boats and barges glide by. Remembering our last evacuation episode on the Volga, I dozed off until the jolt of the boat as it bumped against the far pier woke me with a start.

At around six, we set off on our long trek home. The walk was much easier, not because carrying the heavy shopping bag on my back was any easier, but because I had triumphed over my own physical limitations, over the bureaucrats in the grocery store and over the crisis in my family. The good women kept chatting on the way back, while I walked ahead, contemplating the sunset. Just as it had that morning, the sun played hide and seek behind the mountains, but on the other side this time. As we approached the village, I thanked my companions for their help and promised to repay them the money I had borrowed as soon as possible.

"I'm not worried about that, son," interrupted Fedora. "This is our house. Tell your mother that you haven't betrayed our trust in you, or hers. Goodnight!"

After bidding them goodbye, I stood still at the gate and watched until they clattered into the house. The world is not without good people, I thought, as I approached our castle. As soon as I knocked on the window, Yosif ran out and, taking my bag, asked, "So, how was the game?"

"A draw," I said in reply to his chess reference.

"Good. The main thing is you're back in one piece. Mum's been really worried, cursing herself all the time for allowing you to go."

She threw her arms around me in the hallway. "Oh, thank God! Thank God!"

"Mummy, everything's fine, stop worrying. It's me, Misha, your Golden Middle – don't you recognise me?" I said.

"So I see," she said through her tears. "First of all, let's go and warm your little bones in hot water. Then you can eat some of your favourite borscht, and you'll feel a lot better."

How did she know that my whole body was racked with pain? It must have been maternal intuition, feeling her child's suffering even at a great distance. It must also have been because of her life experience: bearing four children, enduring three evacuations in three years of war all alone with three youngsters and undergoing two serious operations. Such scars are bound to leave their mark.

I sat in a barrel up to my neck in hot water while my brother kept adding more from the kettle. In the meantime, our mother brought me some warm clothes and helped me climb out. While I was having my 'spa bath', she unpacked the bag and laid the contents out in full view – probably to show Yosif the value of his brother's self-sacrifice in the cause of our well-being. I wolfed down the restorative borscht and told everyone about my adventures, omitting the episode of my fainting on the ferry; there was no point in upsetting Mother more than she was already. She was relieved to hear about the grocery store manageress's offer to redeem our ration tokens at the beginning of every month, because it meant that my trips to town would not have to be so frequent. She decided to thank Fedora herself, repay the loan and discuss arrangements for my monthly expeditions thereafter. She said something else, but I could barely keep my eyes open from exhaustion. Before sleep, Mother deeply massaged my neck, back and calf muscles. I slept like a log, of course. The next morning, she rose before me to get me ready for school on time. It was not as difficult to get to school on my bike as it would have been on foot, since my calves were still aching. Even I found it hard to believe I had walked so far the previous day, carrying so much weight. It must have been what they call a new lease of life.

Chapter 7

EXPLORING ARTISTIC TALENTS

Boys from various forms had been looking for me during break the previous day in order to join the dance club. The advert inviting them to go and register with Zina had been up for two days, but none of them had the confidence to deal directly with a girl. The committee had therefore replaced Zina's name with mine, and told the mums about my compelling rendition of the gypsy dance in the sports hall the previous week. Meanwhile, Zina and her friends were actively spreading the same rumour in every class to increase their chances of finding a partner for the pair dances. I registered everyone's name and promised to help all those who survived the instructors' trials during the next day's rehearsal, with the prospect of a popular sailor dance being devised especially for the boys for the end of year concert.

Soon after classes on the Friday, I met the instructors to familiarise myself with the trial routines, which were designed to test the boys' rhythm, physical coordination and muscle memory. As I would demonstrate each routine for them to copy, I had to perform every tap routine to music myself, so that the candidates could see how they should look and sound. The instructors would observe, and pick out anyone with stage potential; we fully expected some participants to decide not to take things any further. At about two o'clock, I went into the changing rooms to find a motley collection of eleven boys looking neat in their sports kit, and ready to put their dancing talents to the test. Aged between ten and thirteen, they all seemed quite calm, if a little apprehensive. I assured them that there was no need to worry, since I'd be demonstrating every movement with musical accompaniment, and would then repeat the routine together with them; the third time, it would be up to the boys to perform it on their own, with the opportunity to correct their own individual mistakes. I explained that the most important thing was to be self-confident and not look like an idiot. Nervously, they laughed back. "Onwards and upwards, warriors!" I exhorted them as I flung open the door to the sports hall.

Although the trials went much better than I expected, I sensed that the instructors were not very enthusiastic about this project. Either they were concerned about maintaining discipline with boys (a problem they had come across before), or it was a matter of the limited time available. In any case, one of the original eleven candidates left out of shyness, another had no sense of rhythm and a third was just physically wrong. The eight who were left sat on the floor in front of the musicians, trying to remember the training programme, the rules of behaviour with female partners and all the other aspects of training as part of the ensemble. They watched the female dances with interest, and my own separate movement sequences of the sailor dance.

"Do you think we'll ever manage to do that?" one asked.

"Not straight away – but in a couple of months, definitely!" I said, speaking for the instructors.

The domra player agreed to my suggestion that she should help them work with the boys, especially in between rehearsals, on other days during the week.

At the end of the lesson, after the trials, the musicians, Zina and I discussed our solo repertoire, and decided we would start with the comic Russian dance. Zina and I agreed to practise our own movements and pair combinations independently, to save time. Then we would use these fragments as part of the choreography devised by the instructors. Thanks to her domineering mother, Olya, Zina managed to commandeer the sports hall for our personal rehearsals from two till four on Monday and Saturday afternoons, and on Thursdays for my Sailor dance work with the boys. It appeared that both Olya and the parents' committee were worried that we'd soon return to Odessa, thereby depriving their children of this opportunity to be educated in dance, so they did everything to make the most of their good fortune.

At the last chess session, Andrey had conveyed his mother Paulina's invitation to lunch with them on the following Sunday. I promised to be there at twelve. It was a very warm reunion. On the way, I picked a bunch of flowers that grew near their house, as I couldn't go empty-handed. Paulina kissed me with tearful affection and Andrey's little sister kept insisting on playing pat-a-cake with me, as we had often done when I was staying with them. Over lunch, Paulina asked, "Misha, is it true you went to sell potatoes in town, with Fedora's family?"

I was so surprised, I almost choked. "Why? Is that a crime?"

"No, on the contrary. I'm just proud that I had such a brave adoptive son, at least for a while."

"Why 'had'?" I asked. "You'll always be Mummy Paulina, and longshanks Andrey will always be my brother."

"And what about me?" cried the three-year-old.

"And you – you'll always be my darling little sister." Everyone smiled.

"You're a good egg, Misha." The lady of the house proclaimed everyone's delight with the true Musketeer.

"Who? Who?" asked the little girl. "Let's go, I'll explain it in your room."

After lunch, while Paulina was putting her daughter to bed for a nap, Andrey and I sat down to a chess game. I had left the set there as a keepsake of my stay. As she walked past us on her way from the bedroom to the kitchen, Paulina whispered to me, "After this game, can we talk business?" I nodded, while carrying on with the game.

"Mum, you're distracting us," complained her son, before declaring "Check!"

After the game, I said I missed the goat and the wicked cockerel. "The goat often thinks of you. As for the cockerel, we ate him at Easter."

"Oh, no!" I said, "Poor hens!"

"They actually went on strike in protest against his poor service." I couldn't help sniggering.

"We have a new Casanova, now. He won't let anyone near his harem."

Paulina approached and gestured an end to our chat. She sat opposite us, waited for the chess set to be put away and without further ado, grabbed the bull by the horns.

"Misha, you know in June, a couple of months before the vegetable crop is ready to harvest, all the village families find it hard, especially nowadays. We also have potatoes and beetroot to sell and Andrey doesn't want to do it all by himself, but is willing to do it with you. We have a two-wheel handcart that my husband and I, she sighed deeply, used every spring to take our surplus produce to sell at the Zhiguly cooperative. It helped us make ends meet until the following harvest. Ask your mother what she thinks. It'll be much easier to drag the cart with two of you, and it can take not just two, but eight buckets full of vegetables. Besides, it's a lot more fun, and safer, if both of you go together, rather than on your own."

"Mother Paulina, to be honest, I was thinking of just that on my way to Kuybyshev, but was too embarrassed to offer our decrepit three-wheel barrow. Tomorrow, I'll let you know Mum's decision. I'm sure she'll say yes."

At six the next morning I was already standing on the porch with my load, fully prepared. When Andrey and Paulina appeared, I knocked on the door to tell Mother. While the women exchanged pleasantries, my partner and I spread out our sacks of potatoes evenly on the cart and went to catch up with our travelling companions, who were starting out from the other side of the village. When they saw the two of us manoeuvring the cart so easily, the women greeted us noisily, with comments to the effect that with such men at their side, they would not fear the devil himself. Three of the women turned out to be relatives of Andrey's father, and they were glad to have our company.

"This is Misha," said my companion. In reply, the three women gave their names in unison, making it impossible to catch a single one. Andrey and I burst out laughing.

"What's with you?" they asked.

"What's with *you*?" I joked. Now it was their turn to roar with laughter. "Our Paulina was right. You really are sharp for your age, child."

"We do our best, ladies."

The cart had a crossbar with two handles. Even though we kept having to swap hands, we walked quite fast. The market opened at seven thirty and trading started at eight. The two of us easily unloaded and laid out our things on a stall near the relatives. We sold everything on ours before they did, probably because customers had more sympathy for children helping their parents.

Andrey told the women that he wanted to show me the town of Zhiguly, and that we'd be back in half an hour. He asked them to keep an eye on his cart and, just in case, tied one of the wheels to the leg of their stall. The town didn't look very big, but was neatly laid out over hills and built in traditional architectural style. It transpired that it had been a centre of historical interest ever since the bloody Mongol invasions of Genghis Khan.

Mother was happy to see me looking energetic and healthy again, and thanked me for buying the items on her shopping list. She couldn't wait to hear how I'd been received by Andrey's relatives. I had to answer all her questions over dinner. I had even bought a spinning top as a present for my little brother. He didn't forget to thank me, and basked in Mother's praise as a result. I asked her how much longer we would have to do these walks, because school exams were approaching, as well as getting ready for the concert and the chess tournament in which Andrey and I were taking part.

"Four more trips, I think," she said, calculating the dates on the calendar.

Nevertheless, the country's economic situation was deteriorating by the day. The Red Army kept advancing, liberating our cities, where the inhabitants had nothing left to eat. The armed forces were always given priority. Civilians had to tighten their belts yet another notch. Mother's allowance was for 500g of bread a day and we boys had 300g each. The shelves in the village shop were conspicuous by their emptiness. Mother worked wonders with potatoes: purée, soup, pancakes; she fried them, steamed them or, better, served them in a salad with onions and pickles. After a while this diet became unbearable. At the kindergarten, parents and cooperative farm managers would sometimes give a little something but, on his off days, Roman would boycott potatoes, eating almost nothing except tea and dried bread for two days. From 1st April, our mother began receiving her invalidity pension in addition to father's, for the children. For the first time in a long time, things did not seem so bad, financially speaking. In reality, however, there was nothing you could buy with that money. We managed to survive only thanks to my trips into town, where – provided you paid three times the price – a few things could be bought.

To save her cubs, our Bagheera turned to crime. She began to 'lend' other housewives the flour and grain that had been lying in the cellar for years. Yosif and I knew full well the origin of the delicacies on our table, but decided not to raise the subject. I must admit that the pearl barley porridge and the onion and potato dumplings managed not to stick in our throats, but Mother always found an excuse not to sit at table with us during those occasions.

Our commander once again summoned us to explain the national and local economic situation.

"All the neighbours have already cleaned and dug out their vegetable patches, and have started sowing seeds and putting in cuttings. So now, Dusya has arranged with the school parents' committee to organise a team of volunteers among the older pupils to come and clear our patch next week. Sidor and other invalids like him will also need help. Although this is officially only for fifth to seventh form children, it'll look bad if you two don't play a leading part in the team."

On the volunteering day, Mother baked about two hundred potato and cabbage pies for the occasion. After two hours of rowdy work, my brother and I triumphantly brought out two huge pots of hot pies and six litres of bread kvass. Everyone devoured the delicious treat, and drank straight from the bottles.

Attracted by the noise, old Sidor came over. "Is it a wedding? Why wasn't I invited?"

"Because there are only two brother-grooms for us twenty-three girls," the eldest of the girls joked. "Now you're here, that makes three."

Then, as everyone laughed, she gave the confused old man a kiss. Mother brought him some pies and a mug for the kvass, and I dragged out the stool and made our dear guest sit down. After the snack, the merry band of girls followed the old man to clear his vegetable patch, thanking the lady of the house for the unexpected feast as they left.

The next job was to dig up our patch and sow the vegetables and tend them. Our commander knew that all the housewives had worries of their own. At the peak of the sowing period for both the collective farm and private vegetable patches, free helpers were in short supply. Nevertheless, she offered this project to Fedora's brigade to take on, for a fixed sum, in their spare time outside their main workload. As a representative of the authorities, Dusya could not be seen to be involved in this operation, so Mother acted independently. She decided that, exceptionally, she would spend her invalidity pension on paying for this work that she could not handle herself. Fedora and her daughters agreed, giving Mother one less thing to worry about regarding our future food supply.

My newly-minted terpsichoreans were making slow but steady progress. In great detail, I practised Russian steps, taps, squats and claps with them. The boys found the latter the hardest. The ordinary handclaps in front were combined with a light tap with one hand on the sole of the foot or just above the knee, while the other was held up high or to the side, for balance. My novices were more successful at performing the purely physical tricks, such as crouching with knees wide apart, even competing among themselves. But the handclap was more complicated, since it demanded several things at the same time: a good sense of rhythm, precise coordination of head and limb movements, balancing on one leg and the ability to assume expressive poses, all in a very intense, emotional dance.

It was important for me to prepare the boys psychologically as well as physically and technically before they could be paired up with their more experienced female partners, especially as most of them had not yet experienced any kind of intimacy with a member of the opposite sex. This was a critical milestone for them, and Zina came to my help yet again. In line with the system we had worked out, she would start off by demonstrating the various elements of the duet with me. Then she would grab hold of the next boy, place his paws on her waist and spin with him, or make him lift her during a leap.

I tried without success to calm down the boys sitting on the floor. Every time one of them danced with Zina, the others would fall back, start wriggling their legs with glee and neighing like horses. On hearing this commotion, the headmistress came in.

"What is going on, here?" she demanded.

"Zina's training future partners how to dance with the girls."

"Well, just make sure it's done a little less noisily," she retorted, barely able to conceal her own amusement.

Finally, the day arrived for the boys and girls to dance together. The instructor who had been preparing the girls had obviously done a good job, since they behaved with discipline and assurance. They showed both initiative and patience in their contact with their inexperienced partners, unaffectedly taking the boys by the hands and pressing their palms against their own waists, and placing their own hands on the boys' shoulders. I had already forewarned the other boys that in traditional pair dances, the woman usually carries the theme and the interactions, while the man demonstrates his confidence and male dignity by always controlling his physical contact with his partner.

The accordionist played, while the domra player led the rehearsals. She placed Zina and me at the head of two lines with four couples in each, and we started to learn the hand positions of Russian folk dancing. We had to overcome the boys' psychological resistance to this first close contact with girls. At first, Zina and I demonstrated, while the others copied. The instructor circulated among the pairs and, gently so as not to intimidate them, corrected them, particularly the position of the boys' hands. Zina and I then showed the triple step with pause, holding hands: going forward, then back. For the final exercise, we raised our right hands, clasped, and walked around each other clockwise. Thankfully, the boys' physical closeness with unknown partners was by then unimpaired by giggling impropriety on either side.

While we were at school, Fedora went to see Mother to make arrangements about scheduling the work to be done, the types of vegetable and their order of planting. Mother was happy to hear that we would now have our own radishes, carrots, onions, cabbages and other green vegetables from the first planting, as well as potatoes and beetroot from the second, in July.

Fedora agreed to get the seeds and cuttings ready the following Sunday, while her daughters were digging up our whole vegetable patch; after lunch, they would sow the first batch of vegetables. In the meantime, they would take it in turns every day to prepare the soil – weeding, trimming, everything except watering. That was something my brother and I would have to do, since our helpers had to work at the collective farm on weekdays. Once again, our commander called a family council, and Yosif and I allocated three days a week each when we would water the seedlings, swapping days if need be.

The choreographers devised a comic Russian dance called 'The Doll and the Jester with a Balalaika' for Zina and me. It was a technically complex routine, with tricks and comedy. In the finale, Zina leaned on my shoulders and leapt up high into the air, bending her legs back, and I lifted her by the waist above my head. Fortunately she was as light as a feather, and my training with the sacks of potatoes on my shoulders certainly helped. Once I had spun around with her, I dropped down on my bottom, spreading my legs and opening my eyes wide; the doll then stood over me, hands on hips, and shook her head at me. Zina particularly liked this final gesture of female supremacy, as did her mother, Olya. I forgave them, because I loved them both. My partner and I also had some solo variations with a chorus of girls in the girls' dances, and pair routines to the accompaniment of a mixed choir. After some tweaking, this made for a very effective finale.

I visited old Sidor every week when I went into town or the district centre to ask if he needed anything done, such as shopping. He always replied that he was well looked after by his daughter-in-law or his niece. He asked how we were getting along with his bicycles, and if our mother needed him to help her around the house.

I put his mind at rest. "It's all fine for the time being. Thank you."

Clearly, the old man was gradually surrendering, but I didn't know what to do to help. Dusya told Mother that they had recently learned that his eldest son had been killed. Sidor himself had not been told, since all he lived for was the hope of seeing his victorious sons after the war. But men as old as he was possess an uncanny instinct, which is why he looked so downhearted. Truth will out, as they say – one day, someone in the street unintentionally broke the news by offering condolences for the loss of his son. The next morning, Sidor didn't wake up. He had died of a broken heart. I was devastated by the loss of such an exceptionally kind man, our friendly jack-of-all-trades. We were now short of a protector.

Chapter 8

THE AGONIES OF FAMILY SURVIVAL

From 1st April 1943, the village shop was closed down, since no more goods were being delivered. This meant that there was no longer anywhere in the village for us to redeem the food ration tokens Dusya gave us. The local authorities arranged for the tearoom to hand out a daily ration of bread to every family. Our potato supplies were running low, but we declined the neighbours' free offer of help; for us, scrounging was out of the question. Our mother could find no way out of this impasse. We simply had to find a way of surviving two more months until June, when the new crop on our vegetable patch would be ready to harvest.

When we innocently asked Dusya why no more goods were being delivered to the village shop, she explained it to us in layman's terms: "It's because of the regions bordering Europe were occupied so early on, with the wholesale destruction that involved. Our agricultural resources in Asia are exhausted. Speculators are robbing the food stores and selling everything for three times the normal price on the black market. What little miraculously remains is requisitioned for the army and the military hospitals. The fact is, we civilians have nowhere to turn for help. We have to overcome this crisis on our own."

After considering various unworkable ways out of these difficulties, I went to see Paulina with a proposition: "We've got almost no potatoes left to sell, but we've accumulated a lot of food ration tokens that can now only be redeemed in Kuybyshev – and even then, with difficulty. My acquaintance, the grocery store manager, promised to help our family in case of extreme necessity. I suggest that Andrey and I go to town one more time with Fedora's brigade on the Wednesday during the spring holidays, just to sell your vegetables. All we earn will be yours. What I'd get in return is the slim possibility of redeeming these useless ration tokens, and bringing back the shopping my family needs on your cart. That's why it may make sense to take the second trip of the month to Kuybyshev market rather than Zhiguly. What do you think? I'm sure this extra trip will help our families survive this critical period before the new harvest. Don't feel you have to change your plans – it's just a friendly suggestion for you to judge on its merits. I won't be upset if you turn it down."

"Misha, is this your idea, or your mother's?"

"Mum doesn't know anything about it. I need to hear what you think first."

"All right, I'll talk to my son, and he'll let you know what we decide."

The next day, Andrey arrived on his bicycle and said his mother agreed to five trips to town: three in April and two in May. We spent the first day of our vacation playing chess before lunch; afterwards, we went to the mountains to enjoy the spring scenery. By the streams, there were many birds that I'd never seen before. They built their nests above the steep mountain precipices of the mountains and came to feed by the water. Bathing there was impossible, because of the sharp stones in the muddy riverbed. Even so, it was a little corner of paradise and I could see why my friend had brought me there. He and I were the same age and even though I was now in a different form, our friendship had not ended – quite the contrary.

In the winter of 1943, demoralised by their defeat at the gates of Stalingrad and by the bitter cold, the enemy forces were retreating in a panic. But in the spring, Hitler sent his tank divisions from Europe to Russia and temporarily slowed down the advance of the Red Army. For obvious reasons, the Soviets hesitated to open a second front. In military terms, this decision determined whether or not Odessa would be liberated that year; realistically, we would most probably have to stay here for another year. Mother was beside herself; there was no news at all from father. Food was increasingly short. Our last hope, my trips to Kuybyshev, would be over by the end of May. After that, we would be busy preparing for

217

our exams, and for the end of year concert. Where, and from whom, would our family get food, was a question that tortured Mother; even she, in all her wisdom, could find no way out of this impasse, and she was fading away before our very eyes. The situation simply could not go on. I told my brother we had to talk, but he replied that he had no time for chitchat.

"In that case, tomorrow, instead of bread, you can chew your fingers!" I spat, walking away towards the shed. He grabbed me by the shoulder and yanked me towards him. "Are you trying to threaten me, you dancing cripple? Just wait till I..."

He did not finish his sentence, because I kneed him hard in the groin. "I've already warned you. Next time, I'll mash your pathetic little nuts to a pulp."

Crouching in pain and nursing his jewels, he let fly a stream of expletives at me. Mother, pale, came to see what the hubbub was about.

"What happened, Yosif?"

"Nothing. I'll deal with the little bastard myself."

"Mum, your chess king can walk all the way to town with Fedora to do the shopping on Wednesday – I'm going to school. I'm sick and tired of feeding this freeloader. I'm not the family lackey anymore."

I grabbed the bicycle and went to see Andrey. When I came back that evening, I wished everyone goodnight and went straight to bed. I don't know what went on between Mother and my brother after our row the previous day, but before school the next morning, he caught me at the gate and said we absolutely had to talk. I threw his own words back at him: "I don't have time for chit-chat."

"I didn't know what you were going to say," he mumbled, his tail between his legs like a beaten dog.

"All you had to do was ask, instead of always rejecting suggestions before even listening to see if they're any good or not."

"All right, all right, so I lost my temper. But that doesn't give you the right to ruin my entire sex life for ever. Let's meet at five behind the shed, as usual."

I gave him a nod and rode off in a rush so as not to miss my first class. On the way, I was upset. On the one hand, I had to force this selfish brother of mine to stop thinking just about himself – especially as he was the eldest. As the man of the house, it was his task more than his brothers' to take care of the whole family, as well as us individually. On the other hand, I was worried about Mother's condition. If I now stopped fetching food for our family because of him, she wouldn't be able to bear it. I had to find the solution to making my brother change his attitude.

"So this is how it is, my dear brother," I began without ceremony. "Everybody knows you're very busy with studying, with chess, the library and your own private business. However, you've forgotten your family responsibilities as the eldest son of the household. You don't care where the food you scoff every day comes from, or the soap in the bathroom, or the new socks, or anything else for that matter. You haven't asked me once how I feel after walking twenty-four kilometres to the town market and back, just so I can redeem ration tokens – including yours – and get Mum's medicine."

My brother tried to interrupt me, but I pressed on. "Starting from 1st June, Andrey and I will be busy with school exams, just like you, and won't be able to go to market. So where's the food on our plates going to come from? That's the issue. We're going to have to tighten our belts even more until the end of June."

Yosif raised his hand sarcastically, "And might I ask how I'm supposed to be the family's saviour under these circumstances? In practice, what exactly do you and Mother actually want from me?" he asked indignantly.

"May I answer?" I said, preventing him from launching into his favourite tirade about all our troubles stemming from the mistake of our evacuation. "First of all, stop being such an arsehole. You know perfectly well what we're talking about here. Of course, it's much easier for you just to come home where everything is laid on, so you don't have to get your soft little hands dirty, like you did in Odessa. Secondly, it's not up to the eldest brother to ask the younger what he should do, but to give advice himself when the family runs into difficulties. Today, at the end of April, I'm giving you notice that during July and August – so for the whole summer – I've enlisted as a ship boy on a freight barge on the Volga. I'll have to wash the deck with a hose every day and scrub the equipment. In return, I'll get a cabin and three meals a day. It'll be up to you to take care of our family then."

"That's betrayal!"

"It's only what you've been doing to this family for the past two years."

After dinner, our mother called me and asked why I had taken work as a ship boy on a barge. I asked her to hear me out without interrupting and signalled with my eyes towards the door behind which Yosif was sure to be skulking (as I would have done in his place).

"Mummy, much as I love you and Roman, I don't want to sacrifice my own interests, my health and my time, for the benefit of this parasite in the family. He behaves as though the world owes him a living. I understand that, as a mother, you have to put up with everything from your children but why is it always me, two years younger than he is, that's always taking the initiative to sort out our problems, while all he does is reap the rewards? It's simply unfair, as I've told you before."

I deliberately raised my voice, so that Yosif wouldn't miss any vital information on which to decide his next steps. "I'm sorry Mum, but why do you let him get away with ignoring his responsibilities as the man of the house, like in any other family?"

"Misha, I don't have the strength to fight with the two of you. If your brother refuses to acknowledge that manna doesn't fall from heaven, he must take responsibility for his selfishness. I agree that when the academic year ends,

Yosif must take your place on the trips to town with Fedora for two months to fetch the supplies we need. Not just to be fair to you – the exercise will be good for him physically, too. But I'm in no position to force him to do it. He'll simply have to go hungry and get ill, that's all. What I want to know is, what exactly are you going to do over the summer?"

"Officially, as you know, nobody will employ me at the age of eleven. I have a few irons in the fire, and being a ship boy on a barge is one of them. If I can, I want to find work in exchange for bed and board at least, so I can support myself and the family budget has one less mouth to feed. Many boys at school do it, with their parents' permission. And on top of that, it would be good life experience for me."

From 1st June, I devoted all my energies not just to my exams and marked assignments, but also the final rehearsals of the dance ensemble, which provided a welcome diversion from all my academic studies in class. I was very pleased with my work with the boys. They performed the simple sailor dance with great enthusiasm – a great achievement, given that they were beginners. They performed all the basic handclaps in the rows of sailors and the triple-step in a round neatly and in time with one another. The hardest thing for them was to keep memorising my example in order to reproduce it for the audience: the sweeping gestures of the sailors, their swaying movements on the rough seas, the humour both on their faces and in their mime poses – all the

222

characteristics that differentiate the sailor's dance from other thematic compositions.

The most visible progress was in my performance with my perfect partner. In Odessa, I had done little more that wriggle my feet on my own – so much so that they nicknamed me 'wriggler'. But dancing around on your own to familiar movements or improvising on the spot is quite different from dancing to a rigid set of sequences and to a pattern of wider movements in a couple. There's the distribution of rhythms over the duration of the dance, the fixed poses and hand holds and so on, and above all, the on-stage spiritual connection between two performers acting as one, emotionally as well as technically. On that front, Zina could not forgive even the tiniest mistake in either herself or in her partner. Without realising it, she instilled the imperative of total self-control and inner impulse into our partnership.

At the end of the exams, on the last Saturday in June, the customary parents' meeting was announced, followed by the long-awaited concert for those taking part. The sports hall was transformed into an auditorium with a stage at one end. There was a dress rehearsal from morning until lunchtime. First, the choir and folk orchestra, followed by the dance collective with the orchestra. The headmistress started the parents' meeting at six, reporting on the past year's results and the plans for the next. She remarked upon the success of both the chess club and the dance group. When she had finished, the parents' committee reminded us that, under their supervision, the library and sports hall would be accessible in the afternoons over the summer. Bringing the meeting to a close, the headmistress invited everyone to the concert. Yosif managed to bring our little brother over on time, but there were no more seats left in the hall. Sitting in the front row, Olya just grabbed him and placed him right next to her.

My presentation began with the Doll Duet. With my Russian doll waiting for me on stage, I took my colourful balalaika and whirled it around histrionically to set a happy mood. I slid my jester's cap and tassel down sideways on my head; I checked the plaited belt on my side, then squatted a few times to warm up my legs. I pulled a grimace to force a smile out of my stern partner. The music started and Zina, wearing her vast pinafore and looking at me with indifference, proudly floated in a whirl. I followed her, still crouching, doing the goose step. Leaning back, I once again mimed playing the balalaika, smiling from ear to ear. The audience fell silent, expecting something extraordinary. After coming out, the doll took a deep bow, and I straightened up to my full height of one and a half metres. The doll began to spin, swaying from side to side. My jester continued his musical 'accompaniment' moving around her enthusiastically with a side step, tapping on the cut-out plywood balalaika. There followed a succession of variations on Russian steps and playful tricks in the form of a contest – in all, a collection of brightly coloured comic scenes and the virtuoso tricks of two young performers. The audience had obviously never seen such rich choreography in folk dancing.

The concert concluded with 'Venzelya', a reel for couples. The boys led out their partners to the loud accompaniment of parental applause. The mothers found it touching to see their usually unruly brats dancing so well, holding a girl by the hand. Many could not believe their eyes; some even became quite tearful. The spatial patterns varied according to the music, the couples weaving and spinning in perfect unison, making a deep impression on the audience. In the finale, Zina and I and the other dancers joined the reel and performed together as a complete school ensemble. The applause went on and on. My little brother kept clapping after everyone else had stopped. He was one of the first people to come up on the stage and shake Zina's hand and mine, congratulating us. The artists mingled with the guests. The headmistress thanked the instructors, and congratulated them on the successful result of their work. I was sad that, because the school was so far away, our mother could not see her son's moment of triumph.

Coming out of the changing rooms, I bowed to all the other mothers waiting for their children. They congratulated me, and wished me well for the holidays. Out of the blue, I was stopped by Olya, who kissed me on the forehead as usual, grateful for the entertainment she had enjoyed. She dragged me to the nearby cart and introduced me to her elderly parents.

"This is Misha – Zina's friend and dance partner."

While Olya went to look for her daughter, the old people asked me about Mother's health, and when we were planning to go back to the Ukraine. I shrugged.

"It all depends on when Odessa is liberated from the occupying forces; next year, I hope."

"Do you like our district?" asked the chairman.

"Very much," I smiled, "but it's not like home." At that moment, their granddaughter came running.

"Misha-Clown, congratulations and thank you very much for being so patient with me." She kissed me on the cheek and hopped onto the cart. I theatrically clasped my hand over my cheek, opened my mouth and started to blink. Everyone burst out laughing.

"What's the matter, Misha dear? Aren't you used to this yet?" enquired Olya.

"On the stage, yes – but in real life, this could be quite dangerous," I answered to general laughter.

"All right, Musketeer. Give our regards to your mother, and come for lunch with us tomorrow at twelve," purred Olya, stroking me behind the ear.

"Yes, Comrade Commander!" I shouted in their departing wake.

As I cycled back home, I kept thinking of Mummy. If I left her on her own with parasite Yosif and with my little brother at weekends, she would not be able to bear this suffering for two whole months. I had to do everything in my power to force him to help our family. My eldest brother had to go into town once a week to redeem the ration tokens. Otherwise, he would totally take advantage of us and start bossing everyone around. I could not allow that to happen; I simply had to find a way out of this impasse. What if I spoke to Olya the next day about the possibility of my working part-time at the collective farm until the school holidays were over, with payment in food rather than money? The chairman knew me now, which would help her persuade her father if she thought it a real possibility. That way, we would at least have eggs, milk, vegetables and fruit for the entire summer. And importantly, I would be close by in case anything happened to Mother again. Come on Misha, once more into the breach!

A mother is always a mother. Hearing about our success from Roman, she prepared to greet me. She congratulated me with a kiss and told me to hop into the barrel of hot water to freshen up and relieve the tiredness. I conveyed the greetings from the chairman's family and told her I had been invited to lunch the next day to celebrate the successful end of the dance season with Zina. Over dinner, I told her every detail about the performance, the boys and their parents.

"They asked me why my mother hadn't come to the meeting and the concert. I told them it was too far to walk and you weren't strong enough yet after your last operation."

Mother looked sadly into my eyes for what seemed a long time. "I'm sorry son, but I don't have anything to wear to social occasions. Good night."

I felt my face burn. What an idiot! Of course, she had been wearing the same old clothes she had worn back in Odessa for three long years, and had bought almost nothing new. Why hadn't it occurred to me? A distinguished woman wearing old rags. The only thing she had allowed herself was a pair of warm boots and gloves.

Because of the over-excitement, I could not stop doing the sailor dance in my sleep, egged on by the other boys. I awoke with a start to see my older brother's fierce face in front of mine. He was shaking me by the shoulders. "What's with all the screaming? Let folk sleep, will you!"

I stared at him. Concerned, our mother walked in, holding the paraffin lamp. "Yosif, what's the matter?" she asked.

"He's even singing in his sleep, loud enough for the whole village to hear. It's stopping everyone from sleeping."

"All right, calm down both of you, and try and go back to sleep," she whispered, turning down the lamp. It was a long time before I got back to sleep. I couldn't stop thinking how cruel my own brother was, to start such a scene when I was fast asleep in the middle of the night.

In the morning, I swept the yard so that my little brother could play football, made myself handsome in front of the mirror and went to lunch. Zina had only just woken up. Having played in the orchestra in the first part of the concert then danced in the second half, she was so tired that her mother had left her to sleep. I immediately sat at the piano and warmed up my fingers with various arpeggios. I tried to pick out tunes I had heard the orchestra play the day before, and tried to remember the Moldavian suite. I began with the adagio, switched to the andante, returned to the lyrical Romance and completed the sequence with a passionate allegro. Someone applauded just behind me.

"What's that?" Zina and her mother asked in unison.

"A Romano-Moldavian rhapsody," I replied, wistfully.

"How do you know all these beautiful melodies?" continued Olya.

"My mother was born in Bessarabia, not far from Odessa. It used to be part of Romania. She taught me to speak Moldavian and often sang folk tunes. She even showed me some Romanian movements she used to dance as a girl. I tried to remember everything, then play it on the piano or dance it.

"Misha, do you have the score to this suite?"

"No, but I'm sure our musicians must have it, since I've often heard it played by various folk orchestras. Why are you so interested?" I asked, curious.

"I want you to devise us a dance out of them," she declared firmly.

Touched by this exchange, Olya joined in. "Zina darling, you mustn't just demand things from Mikhail, like that. It's not very polite, since he's here as our guest."

"Mummy," Olya's daughter wheedled, "you're interfering in my relationships with my friends, even though you're promised you wouldn't do it anymore."

"You're right, darling, I apologise. There. I'm gone," said Olya, taking a step back towards the kitchen.

"All right, ballerina. I'm happy to play these melodies for you so you can note down the top line. The accordionist will then arrange the left-hand accompaniments later. Then you can play the main tune with your right hand, and I'll do the harmonies. All right?"

"All right," she confirmed. "Let's do it after lunch."

"At your service, your Honour." I straightened to attention and saluted her.

She slapped me on the arm. "Stop clowning around! I'm not a Russian doll now!"

"Auntie Olya," I whimpered, "your daughter's beating me up!"

"You obviously deserve it," came the reply. "You'll get another slap if you don't stop complaining!"

"Oh my God, where have I ended up? Scout's honour – I'm innocent!"

"It makes no difference," said Olya, peeking into the parlour. "Be thankful you're still alive!

Come on people, come and eat," she said, inviting us into the dining room.

Over lunch, I told some funny stories. Olya was surprised. "Really? Is that possible?"

"Mummy, don't listen to him. He's a miniature Baron Munchausen." We all burst out laughing. Between courses, I popped into the kitchen and asked Olya if she could give me her advice about something personal after lunch, in confidence. She nodded.

"What are you whispering about?" protested her daughter.

"We're declaring our love," I replied without hesitation.

"Is that so?" said Zina, throwing her hands up theatrically. "And I thought you loved me!"

"Oh, I do," I tried to explain. "I love you as an artist. As for Olya Vassilyevna, I love her as..." I went quiet.

"Keep going, Misha, don't be shy," Olya continued the game.

"... As an artist's mother!" I blurted, finally finding an escape route.

We were laughing so loud that the grandmother came in from the other half of the house. Seeing her granddaughter chasing me around the table, and hitting me jealously with her napkin, she asked, "What's this? The continuation of yesterday's concert?"

"Seems like it, Mother. You'll never get bored while you have these scoundrels around. We'd better have some tea," concluded Olya, putting the samovar on the table. After tea, Olya asked her daughter to play something classical for her grandmother while we had a serious talk. She closed the door, and sat opposite me expectantly. I stared into her eyes, and sighed.

"Olya Vassilyevna, we have some serious problems in our family at the moment. As you know, many of the older pupils at school often work at the collective farm or on a building site or somewhere over the summer holidays, to help their families until the next harvest. I also have a chance of getting a place for two months as a ship boy on the barge of a captain I know. However, I'm afraid to leave our sick mother on her own with our problems for so long. I wanted to ask you if there is any possibility I could work half days at the collective farm, so I could spend the rest of the time taking care of chores at home, and doing my own things. Perhaps you've heard of my trips to town to sell potatoes with Fedora? She can vouch for my hard work and behaviour. I've been doing it with my friend Andrey from the third form for the last two months. If I can't manage the workload on my own, we can do it together with his cart; we could work six days a week, mornings or afternoons."

"Wouldn't it be better for you to share the workload with your older brother?"

"Yosif isn't physically very strong and he prefers working with his head more than his hands. Besides, we don't have a cart for transporting the loads."

"What kind of agricultural work do you think you could do at eleven years old?"

"I could collect, transport, sort out and pack fruit and vegetables. I could water part of the crop with a hose. I could carry messages on my bicycle between the management and the workers. Basically, I'd be ready to do any kind of work you think I'd be suitable for. And even if the chairman can't grant my request, that will change nothing in my attitude towards your family. I'll just have to sit on a barge for two months and miss you."

"You go and make music with my daughter while I talk to my father. He may be able to think of some other option. I can't promise you anything, you understand – it's not up to me. Let's hope we manage to work something out."

While Olya conferred with her father, Zina and I were busy transcribing the Moldavian suite. I played the melody in a slow, deliberate tempo, repeating it several times until the phrase was consolidated correctly. It turned out to be quite a fiddly job, but we nevertheless made fast progress, thanks to my partner's perseverance and excellent ear. After we finished the first part of the suite, Olya took me into the kitchen; Zina promised to make a clean copy of our work during my absence. From the expression in Olya's eyes, I could tell that there was some small hope, and I was impatient to hear her news.

"Once again, my father has decided to help your family. He's going to instruct the supervisor to change the method of collecting and sorting vegetables for two months, to meet the demands of the supplementary work force. Before, we had a gang of women gathering the crop all morning, sorting it into crates in the afternoon and carrying them to the side of the road to be picked up by trucks. Now though, you and your elder brother or Andrey will be doing the second part of the work, with the crates. After lunch, the farm workers will move to the next section and you'll follow them as soon as you've finished your previous job. That way, you'll all be working like a conveyor belt."

Feisty Olya went to make the necessary arrangements while Zina and I carried on with our transcriptions. When we had finished with the final part of the suite, we worked out the dance order and decided to try it out together to see how it all sounded. Zina played the melody with her right hand, turning the pages with her left. I used both hands to improvise the harmony to complement the top line. The result was a cacophony to start with, but after a while, we managed to fall into step with each other while trying to maintain the overall composition of the piece with our playing. When she came back home, Olya was overwhelmed by the beautiful music and our interpretation. At the end, she applauded and said she now understood why her Zina was so keen on performing this dance.

Calling me again into the kitchen, my good fairy gave me the details of the job. We had to be at the management office at nine thirty the next morning, without the cart, because they had plenty at the collective farm. However, we had to come on our bicycles, since we would need to get about on them as required. The supervisor (also on a bicycle) would take us to our workstation at ten, introduce us to our colleagues and explain the details and order of what we had to do. We would work on the morning produce until lunchtime;

after the break, we would repeat the same operation in the neighbouring section, with the same team. By the end of our shift, at three, we had to clear all the crates with that day's vegetables from the roadside, take them into the store rooms for sorting according to destination, and find out from the management where and with whom we would have to work the following day. After we had completed our four-hour shift, we would be marked as having done half a day's work, as long as we had followed the correct procedure. I excused myself, saying that I urgently had to visit Andrey.

"Bye, Zina!" I shouted, "Thanks for everything, Olya Vassilyevna!" I kissed her on the cheek, and immediately heard the familiar voice behind me, "And what about me?"

The daughter was standing by the door, her hands on her hips in a threatening manner. I ran up to her, as if quaking with fear, and gave her a kiss on the other cheek, just for a change.

"That's better," she said crossly, looking at her stunned Mother. Running past Olya, I threw up my arms, and said, "Why split up a family?" and disappeared while I still could.

Andrey was not at home, as he'd gone to tie the goat for afternoon grazing. I found him easily and told him about our possible new adventure for the next two months. He listened attentively, scratching the back of his head, "I already have so much work around the house, what with the animals and the vegetable patch. I don't think Mother will agree. I'd really like to try my hand at something new, but I just don't think I can manage to do both."

"I'm in exactly the same situation," I confessed. "I don't have quite as much to do as you, but I still have a lot on my plate. Tell your mother you want to try it out just for next week. If it's all too much for you, then you'll go back to your previous timetable with no hard feelings. I know you have financial difficulties too, so why not take this opportunity to explore local work contacts? Persuade her to stand in for you looking after the animals four or five hours a day. She can't possibly work outside with a young child, but if it's around the house, she can do pretty much everything. The problem is, we have to make a decision today because the management are expecting us at nine thirty a.m. tomorrow. If she turns us down, I'll be forced to work with my brother, which will be ghastly. I'll wait at home for your answer until six o'clock. If it's a no, don't come."

"All right," said Andrey, rushing off to speak to his mother. In my head, I went through the different ways to put this adventure to my own mother, of the possibility of working jointly with Yosif on the collective farm. Even though I had no faith in the idea and had the proposal up my sleeve only as an insurance policy against failure, it was good to be prepared for any surprises from His Majesty. But how could I anticipate his surprises? Either way, I could think of no other compromises.

Much to my satisfaction, Andrey arrived at five o'clock and announced, "Everything's all right. The whole family went to see Olya. Zina played children's songs to my little sister while the mothers discussed your proposal. The chairman told his daughter to make it clear that he was only making this exception to help the evacuee family of a man fighting at the front."

It was blatantly obvious that what was foremost in Olya's mind was her daughter's friendship with me. She knew only too well that this stroke of good fortune could evaporate if we returned to Odessa. What she could not see is just how deeply I too would feel this loss. As we parted, Andrey and I agreed to meet in the management office the next day at the appointed time. We were both pleased with our success.

"Why was your friend here?" asked Mother over dinner. I reported to her that we had been lucky enough to find work at the collective farm over the summer: four hours a day for part-time work, six days a week from ten till four, including travel time.

"In that case, who's going to sweep the garden and water the vegetable patch, then?"

"The same person who's now going to go and redeem the family tokens in Kuybyshev, bring back the medicine for Mother and take the little one to kindergarten and back," I replied without hesitation. My audacity left my brother speechless.

"And you decided all this behind my back, did you? No way!" he shouted, frightening Roman, and bouncing up from the table. "Tomorrow, I'm going to visit the chairman of the village council and tell him how you're trying to exploit me!" he yelled on his way to the bedroom.

Mother warned me that we would swap beds that night. Roman stared at us, not understanding what was going on. She tried to comfort him: "Don't worry, little one, your eldest brother is just very tired after his exams, which he passed with flying colours. He just needs to rest. Tomorrow morning, Misha will drop you off at kindergarten on his way to work. Tonight, he's going to sleep in my bed, while I sleep in his, to help Yosif in case he's ill during the night. Remember, I'll be in the next room."

In the morning, I had breakfast with Roman, took him to kindergarten and promised to come and pick him up on my way back from work. Before we left, Mother managed to slip a wedge of bread into my pocket, for lunch.

Well, he will certainly give her a hard time, today, I worried to myself. What had happened to our Bagheera? Had she forgotten that you have to give as good as you get? She is too ashamed to wash our dirty laundry in public, which he takes advantage of by getting totally out of control. She simply has to find it in herself to restore her power within the family, or we'll all be lost. She used to be a teacher, after all. Back in Odessa, everybody respected her strong will and spirit. Where had it all gone?

A week earlier, just before the holidays, the school nurse had come to check on Mother's health and had said in my presence that she no longer needed to take the medicine. Otherwise, she would become addicted to it and find it harder and harder to give up. Was this the reason she was feeling so weak and lacking in control? Who could help her? Tomorrow, I would go and see Dusya and ask her advice. Things don't get any easier, I sighed to myself as I approached the management office.

As soon as Roman and I had left, Mother woke Yosif up. At first, he protested that it was the first day of the holidays and he wanted to sleep longer, but thought better of it when he heard some half-forgotten traces of the Commander's former tone of authority.

"Dusya will bring this month's pension and food ration tokens in a moment, and we must have a proper talk before she arrives. There's breakfast waiting for you in the kitchen – probably for the last time. Judging from your behaviour last night, you'll be taking care of yourself in every respect from tomorrow onwards." Bagheera's warning was stern. Yosif suddenly remembered the scene over dinner the night before. He dropped his head and went about his morning ablutions. After breakfast, Mother brought everything into the open. For a long time, she held his gaze.

"Last night, you behaved abominably at the table and set an atrocious example to your younger brothers. I'm waiting for you to apologise for such disrespectful behaviour towards me."

"I'm sorry I flew off the handle. It won't happen again," he promised.

"I forgive you, but for the last time. You're welcome to go and complain to whomever you like about your brothers and your mother who, during these unbearably difficult times, expects from you not only help, but some qualities of leadership – since you're the man of the house – necessary for our survival, just as you promised your father."

"But I already take Roman to kindergarten and back every day. I pick up your letters from the post office, and fetch the bread from the tearoom on my way back from school. I chop the logs and fire the stove in the winter. I draw water from the well in the garden. What else do you all want from me? I don't know."

"I want nothing from you if you can't understand for yourself the times we're living in, and the financial situation we find ourselves in – not just as a family, but as the entire Soviet nation. All the families of the fighting men, especially those from the liberated territories are suffering deprivation and hunger while trying to survive this severe crisis. In the same way, as part of this family, you should be taking the initiative by offering to look after other family members' wellbeing as well as your own. And you, the eldest, call this 'exploitation' and shrink from your family responsibilities. I fulfil all my daily tasks keeping house. Misha's working at the collective farm in exchange for food for us all – including you. You should take on the rest of the work for the rest of the summer – all the fetching and carrying, cleaning outside, watering the vegetable patch, redeeming the ration tokens in town, picking up the post and the bread and doing everything else our family needs. You must also think of ways to ensure our safety, just as you do in chess. In case you decide to renounce your family, you'll immediately be taken to an orphanage. They've already suggested more than once that I should send one of my sons to the children's home to save the other two. In my place, you would do exactly the same. To win a chess game, you often sacrifice your queen without batting an eyelid, don't you? You'd better give your future some serious thought, my boy. You need to become reasonable and self-controlled. You need to give up your pre-war attitudes towards this family while father isn't with us. I have no intention of arguing with you anymore. As a mother, I've done my duty by you. You decide, now. Go back to your room and wait until I call you. I'll let you know when Dusya arrives and I want you to say, in front of her, whether you've decided to live with us or at the orphanage. This is a serious question which must be heard in front of a witness."

Half an hour after Dusya arrived, Mother called in her son. Forewarned about the crux of the problem, our protector had been shown the list of Yosif's family duties.

"I agree to carry out all these duties," he said, indicating the paper in Mother's hand, "So long as I don't get new ones every week."

"I see," came the disappointed reply. "Except that no one can tell today what's around the corner, so there can be no guarantees. If fate forces us to move house again, you might have to leave school for a while, or give up your beloved chess temporarily. We'll do whatever is necessary to keep safe without a moment's hesitation, just as we've already had to do more than once in the past two years. You know exactly what I mean. So conditions on your part are out of the question. You have to find ways of making our lives easier of your own accord, just like Misha has done, and add them to your list of jobs in your own hand. That's non-negotiable!"

Yosif was backed into a corner. With Dusya there, he could not throw his usual tantrum but also had no inclination to "sell himself into slavery" (to use his own expression). While he stood there sullenly trying to decide his fate, Mother took ten minutes to write a letter to the village council chairman: "Given the dire material straits in which, we find ourselves as the family of a fighting soldier, I request that my eldest son Yosif be placed in Kuybyshev orphanage. This is to avoid losing my two younger children who also reside at this address. Thanking you for your attention, and hoping that you will be able to help..."

Anna signed it and handed it to Dusya. Once she had read the contents, the latter gave the letter to Yosif so he would read it and sign it to prove that he agreed with the decision. Yet again, he snapped, tossed aside the letter and went to his room. Disheartened, Mother threw up her arms. Dusya gestured her to stop.

"Anna, you mustn't give in to this emotional blackmail," she whispered. "Your son is playing on your maternal feelings. If you back down now, he'll know he can twist you round his little finger. Not only will it not help him, you'll be reinforcing his selfishness, his antagonism towards his brothers and his lack of self-control. This letter is your very last chance – use it to the full."

Dusya took Yosif's list and the letter from the table, walked up to our bedroom and knocked.

"Yosif, open the door. I want to talk to you. It's for your own good" My brother let her in, and locked the door behind her again. Mother couldn't hear what they were discussing, but having known her child for thirteen years, she could imagine. Dusya was like family to us, so Mother didn't mind her taking part in our family drama; on the contrary, we were grateful for the constant help and time she gave us.

They emerged after half an hour. Dusya presented Anna with the sheet of paper listing the jobs, signed by Yosif. That made it a binding agreement. If he failed to fulfil any of his tasks, all Mother had to do was give the word and her letter would be straight on the chairman's desk.

My brother went to her. "I know I'm in the wrong. Forgive me, I just sometimes have a problem controlling myself."

"I don't believe words any more. You're going to have to prove it with actions."

When I came back at four, shattered after my first day at work, I found Yosif in the garden with a broom in his hand. Making no comment, I went into the house and asked Mother what had happened. She gave me a brief summary of the drama that had taken place, and asked me to act as though nothing had happened. Everything was as it is in normal families. I said that I'd go and pick up Roman after tea, but Mother shook her head. "He will do that after he's finished sweeping the garden. Why don't you tell me about your first day at the collective farm, instead?"

I described how Andrey and I were first met with some joking by the women, but when they saw our hard work with the cart and the crates, they started to raise their eyebrows and exchange approving looks. The team leader took us under her wing from the start and warned us against possible mistakes. After work, she praised us and gave instructions for the following day. Andrey was very happy to get away from being in the house.

Yosif brought Roman back and asked Mother if he could go about his own business. "Thank you son, you can go and rest," she replied with her once familiar confidence. Listening to this calm, seemingly banal exchange, I felt as though I was in a box at the theatre rather than sat at our table. How long will this performance last, I wondered. My doubts were interrupted by Roman: "You promised you'd teach me to ride your bicycle."

"What? What's this?" Mother asked, worried.

"Mum," I protested, "Father bought me a little bike for my fifth birthday. Your youngest son will be six in August, and you're still fussing over him like he was still a baby."

"You're right, Misha," said Roman, pulling at my sleeve. "Let's go for a ride."

Mother scratched the back of her head. "Six already? I can't believe it. Seems like I gave birth to him only yesterday and here he is, on a grown-up bicycle already. They grow like bean sprouts."

Mother had to arrange the last stage of the summer operation with Fedora. I advised her to send Yosif in the first instance with an empty rucksack to bring back the shopping from town, but under the strict condition that he would not stray far from his travelling companions. Otherwise, someone could steal his rucksack, beat him up and demand the purse. He had to understand that he would have to do everything Fedora told him to, unquestioningly. If he didn't, she would refuse to take him again, and we would once again be left in the lurch.

"He must promise you that he won't start showing off in front of her, and try to prove that he's independent. Write a note to the manager of the grocery store, telling her that I'm working over the summer, and that my

245

brother is standing in for me for two months. You don't need any medicine anymore, and Fedora will help him buy everything else, as long as he asks her nicely."

In the evening, the Chief and I went to the end of our road and knocked on the gate. The dog appeared first, followed by the mistress. Sitting on the bench, we persuaded our neighbour to save us one more time, and promised that Yosif would follow her every instruction to the letter – and if he didn't, that she shouldn't feel shy about being stern with him.

At five thirty a.m., Mum woke me up and asked me to go to Fedora's with Yosif, so that I could introduce him. As we approached the house, I made a friendly remark about her being a tough sort of woman who was not to be messed with. My brother was in a foul mood for being woken so early, so instead of being grateful for the warning, he snapped back, "You'd better eat your own shit before you start preaching to others."

"Once a pig, always a pig," I replied calmly. At six on the dot, the four women came out, with Fedora at the head. After friendly greetings, I presented Yosif and asked them to help him in the grocery store by introducing him to the manageress I knew. "He's already been given all the other instructions by Mother. Safe journey!"

On my way back home, I was still full of doubts that the Kuybyshev excursion would be a success and over breakfast, told Mother my reservations about my brother's behaviour. She echoed them, and was also worried that our good relationship with the neighbours might be compromised, along with her reputation as a mother. She admitted to her sense of helplessness at not having any power over her eldest, who was growing emotionally distant from the family.

"Mummy, I think you probably lost your influence over him because of your illness but also, the success of the chess training sessions has given him a big head. If we all act together to stop his parasitic behaviour, he'll have nowhere to turn. The instinct to eat every day forces people either to earn money for food or steal it from others. He thinks far to highly of himself to start stealing, so he'll have no choice but to become self-sufficient or starve. You're not the only mother in this situation. Don't worry."

Because it had an extra seat fitted on the frame, I took Roman to kindergarten on my brother's bicycle, knowing full well he would disapprove. I hoped I could bring him back home before Yosif returned from town with Fedora. I went to pick him up earlier than usual, straight after work, partly because I had a nagging feeling that something was wrong, and partly because I was dying to know how the first march to Kuybyshev had transpired. As Roman and I rode up to the house, we heard a loud argument going on between Mother and Yosif. Home already? So early? I was wary.

He had left his travelling companions in town and walked back by himself. As Roman and I appeared, he flew at me, "How dare you take my bike without permission!"

"First of all, it's not your bike," I replied. "It belongs to the late Old Sidor. Secondly, there's no special seat attachment for Roman on my bike. And, thirdly, I was doing your job for you. You should thank me, instead of attacking your own brothers like a rabid dog."

"Stop it, both of you! That's enough!" the Commander cried. I took frightened Roman by the hand. "Let's go and learn to ride a bike." Ignoring Yosif's threats behind my back, I enjoyed hearing Bagheera's fierce growl once again: "If you find it so unbearable to live in this family, go and see Dusya and sign my application to the orphanage! You've embarrassed me in front of the neighbours! You've thrown out half our food rations on your way back! You bought nothing for us with the money I gave you! You broke your promise to obey Fedora and didn't even tell her you were going home on your own! Shall I carry on? Are you happy that you've broken these elementary rules of behaviour, social as well as in our family? Tell me, why do you hate us all so much? You keep pouncing on your own flesh and blood over the slightest nonsense and then apologise for it. And then you go and do the same thing again shortly afterwards, insulting everyone in the family with your tone and your manner. I'm not accepting your apologies anymore. Starting from tomorrow, you'll have your 300g bread ration for breakfast, lunch and dinner, and as many potatoes as you like. You'll cook your own food and clear

248

up after yourself. I forbid you to speak to me or your brothers with that rude and insulting tone of voice. If you dare as much as open that rude mouth of yours to speak to us, I'll slam it shut with this very hand. And now take Old Sidor's bicycle, and go back down to the road where you threw out our food and bring it back home."

Bagheera seemed to be regaining her form.

That evening, before returning home, Fedora knocked on our window. She reported that, right from when they set off, Yosif lagged behind all the way. At first, she had encouraged him to speed up, explaining that they would all be late for the steamer across the Volga unless he picked up the pace. They had waited for him to catch up while they sat to have their break by the road, when Fedora warned him once again that "seven don't wait for one"; if he was late for the steamer, it would leave without him. Yosif said nothing, and was sullen. The women lifted their laden yokes and carried on walking. Seeing what kind of person they were dealing with, they decided to leave him alone. It's no good having a brilliant mathematical mind for chess if you're going to cut yourself off from the real world. Mother Nature does not tolerate her laws being broken.

At the pier, the women kept anxiously looking out for their delayed travelling companion. At the very last minute, just as they were about to depart, my idiot brother finally crawled up at a snail's pace. When they reached town, Fedora showed him the grocery store where I usually redeemed our tokens, and the spot on the market where they traded. She suggested to the young saboteur that he could take a walk around town for two hours until his companions had finished trading, and be back by twelve o'clock sharp. He agreed and went to take in the sights of Kuybyshev. But at midday, Yosif was nowhere to be seen, and Fedora's group began to worry. First, they went to the grocery store and asked the manageress. She told them the boy had been to redeem his tokens two hours ago.

The women went back to the market to look for the lost boy. Wisely as it turned out, the mother comforted the daughters, saying she was certain that their former travelling companion would be back home before them. On the steamer, they confirmed that a young boy with a large rucksack had indeed crossed the river on the earlier trip. Fedora was not surprised by the teenager's appalling behaviour. She was used to the delinquent behaviour of young people and prayed that nothing bad would happen to my brother on his way home or she would never forgive herself for being too weak to refuse to do a good deed. When, as a sensitive Mother and grandmother, she had glanced at Yosif as she met him early that morning, she had instantly formed a negative impression of him but did not have the heart to refuse a neighbour's request.

Anyway, how could she possibly expect two shoots from the same root to be such opposites? When she got off the steamer, she asked a member of staff on the pier if he had seen Roman, and he replied that a boy with a rucksack had asked the way to Vypolzovo. When she heard this, she decided to give up on him; the women decided that the situation was not so tragic after all, and went on their way.

They split into two groups and walked along both sides of the road in case they came across any signs of robbery or violence. After a couple of kilometres, the long-sighted Fedora suddenly noticed a tin of food laying a little way from the road. Picking it up, the women assumed that the unopened tinned courgettes belonged to Yosif, and began searching through the undergrowth by the roadside. When they found a tin of aubergines, they realised that the tired Musketeer must have been gradually lightening his load by shedding weight, and cheered up. Now Fedora's brigade were certain that Yosif was safe and started playing a game of who would be the first to find the chess player's next 'sacrifice'. They laughed all the way back, making fun of their pathetic companion, and did not notice that they had already covered most of the distance.

As they approached the village, they discovered more trophies: a bottle of vegetable oil and a bottle of vinegar sticking out, part-hidden in the grass on the side of the road. The daughters laughed hysterically. Only their mother was sad, sympathising with her neighbour. Fedora put all the things they had found into the same bag and told the young women to go straight home while she went to call on the mother of the hopeless hero.

"Where's Yosif?" she asked. Mother apologised for all the trouble caused and said that her son had gone back while it was still light to pick up all the items he had left on the road. "Anna, we've only just got back. Your eldest betrayed our trust and we didn't see him on our way back at all. He couldn't possibly have got lost, so he's just lying to you – exactly like my grandchildren lie to their mothers. Here's everything your son threw out, and it's better if you don't tell him anything about it today – let him sweat a little."

The next morning, Yosif first took Roman to kindergarten and, on the way back, cycled out of the village to pick up the food from the road. After riding a few kilometres in vain, he became convinced that it was all lost. No player likes to lose a game, especially not if he fails stupidly through over-confidence. Anticipating the moves of your opponent is more complex in real life than it is on a chessboard, where the pieces have more limited options. Not for the first time, Yosif returned home like a beaten dog. His detested broom awaited him by the gate.

Unfortunately, life – especially in wartime – is less about fun and chasing rainbows than about cruel reality. After ten years of pampering before the war, my brother found it hard to alter his selfish nature. He profoundly believed that the world owed him a living, and that everyone was just picking on him. Even after two years of evacuation, he could not adapt to a new way of living. Yet this was only half of what we would have to endure before the war would end. That is what everyone thought. Yosif, however, had shut himself in his own little world and refused to see any need to compromise outside his unbending framework. It was something with which nobody could help him.

Chapter 9

THE FINAL LEG OF THE MARATHON

The summer of 1943 turned out to be a very satisfying one for everyone in our family. When the old lady librarian of the village municipal library died, Dusya gave Yosif a temporary job for three afternoons a week in the library until September. The law did not allow minors to work full time.

During the war, however, this law was often ignored. My older brother also persuaded a few other chess lovers from the sixth form to ride in groups of three or four bikes to Zhiguly market to deliver fresh vegetables from their patches to the wholesale cooperative. With the money they made, they bought food and household items for their families. 'A peasant needs thunder to cross himself and wonder' – and so it was with Yosif. His companions' mothers were very pleased with this venture, both financially and educationally. Every Sunday afternoon, these boys, along with other chess players, would get together at the school. Our mother could finally relax: both her older sons were working, albeit for pennies, and in her eyes, they were contributing emotionally and in spirit to their family and their fellow villagers. It was a win/win.

Every Sunday, I continued to meet up with Zina in the sports hall, where we gradually developed graceful or energetic movements for the Moldavian dances. She was involved in the choreography, and I could tell that she did a lot of practising at home, polishing the complex technique and style of this suite. Feisty Olya would sometimes peek into the sports hall and watch our joint efforts, entranced – I think she would have loved to dance this rhythmic, passionate routine herself. We planned to have a rough draft of our work by the end of eight or ten rehearsals so that, from September, I could concentrate on the boys and the Russian jesters dance. We could then even help the instructors with the staging of the Ukrainian dance for the couples. Meanwhile, Roman was upstairs playing chess with Yosif. Sometimes, just for a change, he would run down to see our 'hopping' (as he put it). He even amused himself trying to copy me, but without success. Dance was obviously not where his future lay.

In August, as agreed with Mother, Fedora's brigade began to clear the vegetable patch of the spring growth and begin to sow autumn root vegetables. Our summer jobs came to an end in September. The new academic year started, but this time we had the advantage of the previous year's experience; it is always easier to walk a trodden path. As usual, Mother fussed around the house looking after us. We studied at our school desks and concentrated on our leisure activities until one day in October we came home after school to find our mother in tears, a letter in her hand. The Centre for Missing Relatives had communicated that our father was in an Uzbek hospital.

All the details were provided. It turned out that Dad had been wounded in the head by enemy shrapnel, and two pieces would be permanently lodged in his skull, right next to his cerebral cortex. He remained unconscious for a long time, and the injury permanently paralysed his left side. The ambulance convoy transporting the wounded from the front to the hospital was bombed, and almost all the documents were burnt. It was not until much later that father regained consciousness, and his memory even later. The administrative staff then recognised his name and pre-war address, and sent the information to the Centre for Missing Relatives.

For us, the news that the head of our family was alive but immobile was happy and sad in equal measure. It took a long time to comfort Mother; hers was a complex reaction to the torture of not knowing for so long, of hopeful waiting, and now of this hope being dashed. She sent us to bed and sat up until late, writing the story of our evacuation to our father. She also wrote to the head of the hospital, requesting information about the true state of the patient and his prognosis. She asked permission to visit her husband when convenient. In the morning, we all signed the letter before it was sent.

About a month later we received a reply from father, enclosing two photographs. In one, he was lying down; in the other, sitting up, supported by a woman doctor. Mother was once again upset by the conclusion drawn by his doctor: "The boys' father is still in the ward for the critically injured because of frequent epileptic seizures. The slightest nervous upset makes the pieces of shrapnel in his head press on the brain, causing such violent fits that even two nurses find it difficult to restrain him to avoid a potentially fatal trauma." In those days, there were no powerful magnetic machines to draw out pieces of metal safely from the brain. Dad knew that he could die at any moment without warning; he couldn't be moved and required twenty-four hour care.

Psychologically speaking, it was also thought inadvisable for children to see their father having epileptic seizures, but I nevertheless insisted that I wanted to accompany Mother to Uzbekistan, as her bodyguard. These plans never materialised.

Three months went by. Yosif's photograph was displayed on the school's board of honour, as one of the best and most active students. Even so, during the autumn break, he and I had to saw and chop the timber Dusya had brought us for fuel. At the same time, Fedora's brigade were digging up potatoes, beetroot and carrots from our vegetable patch. They cleaned them and sorted them into crates, which my brother and I stored in the cellar. It looked as if we would have a wider variety of food in the coming winter than the previous one. At the very least, we wouldn't run out of borscht.

Mother managed her workers like a real farm manager, as you would expect from a former teacher adapting to new life circumstances. Ever hospitable, she plied everyone with tea and fed them with her pies. All the work was completed by the end of the school holidays, when we returned to the grindstone. After the harvest in the Volga region, tinned macaroni and other household items slowly began appearing in the village shop – a pleasant surprise for the New Year.

As in the autumn before, Zina and I worked intensively on our programme for the New Year – this time, with a much more demanding repertoire, with couple work as well group dances. A few more boys from the lower forms joined our ensemble, which meant more work for the instructors. And for me, too. The accordionist arranged the Moldavian suite that Zina and I had transcribed for our duet, and did the same for the jesters' dance, following my stage plan. Now I could work with the boys in peace. The novices learnt the Ukrainian movements for the Gopak with the girls.

The more experienced former 'sailors' were getting to know the technique of Russian grotesque movements, complete with acrobatic elements and tricks. Zina helped me with the beginners, firmly declaring her ambition to become a professional choreographer one day. This made things easier for me, as she was quick to learn my movements and pass them onto the beginners. The aspiring jesters got so carried away with practising that their poor but proud mothers began to complain about furniture breakages at home.

So many new members joined Yosif's chess club that there weren't enough boards to go around. The parents' committee once again went to ask the two chairmen for help. It would have been inconceivable for them not to encourage their offspring's eagerness for personal and intellectual development.

Being larger and more elaborate than before, the forthcoming New Year celebrations required more work. The general mood of victory endowed the occasion with great social significance. High officials from Zhiguly District Council were planning to come and study the experimental mass culture work of the Volga Region School. Zina and I were given the pressing task of staging a youth show, with a sailor's dance and three Russian dances. Determined to give the important guests an appropriately grand welcome, the local management spared no expense to ensure the success of the sports and music clubs. Ten more chess sets appeared out of nowhere. The parents' committee was given funds to make dance costumes. Mothers spent their nights cutting, stitching and gluing to dress their young dancers and freshen up the musicians' well-worn costumes.

All this frenzy went on until the Zhiguly delegation arrived at the school in the morning of the appointed Saturday. They were met by the parents on duty, who took them into the library reading room that had been prepared for the seminar. The regional instructors, who had arrived early, were in the headmistress's office, confirming the running order of the show, the cultural and sporting programme and the ensuing discussion. The formal part of the meeting began at ten, when the District Council representatives talked about the imminent end of hostilities and the necessity to improve public education in every sphere: ideology, pedagogical techniques, practical laboratory work, cultural education and so on. After observing simultaneous games on thirty boards, there were suggestions that there should be more focus on the new method of teaching the ancient game of chess, by combining it with mathematics. To conclude, there was an exhibition of artistic endeavours, including music, singing, dancing and sport. The guests were interested in seeing how these compared with their own schools, where such activities were well established.

In mid-December, a letter dictated by father arrived, thanking us for our good behaviour and for helping Mother. He said he missed his Musketeers and wanted to see how much we had grown. To Mother, he wrote that he was no better but was being actively treated, and trained to walk with a stick. Unaware that we were well used to it, he assumed that because it would be risky to leave children unsupervised during the winter, it would be better for her to go and see him in the spring. If Odessa was liberated by then, we would then be able to return home together. He said he thought of us all the time. Poor father must have lost his sense of reality, and was hoping for the impossible. The chief doctor wrote in his report that the hospital had a room reserved for visiting relatives for up to a week at a time, with full board. The journey to Tashkent took three days each way, so Anna would need two weeks in all to make the trip. The fare was very expensive. She seemed to have little chance of seeing father.

The Red Army had liberated almost all of the Ukraine. When would they give us back our beloved city? We were impatient. Mother comforted us with the wisdom of an exhausted Panther. "Dear children, it's very easy to listen to the solemn voice of a broadcaster or to watch victory salutes. But when it comes to giving us back what was taken by force, there needs to be a show of great strength on our part, and inevitably, there will be more victims. We have to sit tight and wait, without losing hope or losing faith in the fighters who'll liberate our homeland. There's no doubt that they're doing their very best to do their duty, both morally and physically. Let's just send father a letter with our good wishes for the New Year."

The photo reporters from Zhiguly sent us two sets of photographs taken during our last show. We picked out the best ones of my brother at the synchronised chess games, and of me dancing duets with Zina. Mother sent them to Dad with heartfelt wishes for the New Year and, especially, that we meet again in Odessa.

Dusya was glad to offer Yosif the village library job for the two weeks of the school holiday. He did not find it difficult to fill in readers' membership forms and keep a record of books lent and borrowed. In his free time, he would retrieve obscure editions from the cellar and read them in a single sitting. For four hours' work, he earned a small sum that Mother put aside to buy him new clothes for when we returned to Odessa. The important thing was that Yosif was busy with a task that he enjoyed and which benefitted others. The atmosphere in the house dramatically improved.

Roman finished at his kindergarten in the last week of December. Andrey and I agreed to visit each other with our younger siblings every other day to give our mothers a break during the festive period. His little sister was about five, and Roman was six. They got on very well together, and in light of this, our mothers enjoyed a week's freedom and were glad to exchange greetings via their youngest children. In the meantime, Andrey and I played chess and other games. We went sledging on the nearby hills and enjoyed delicious meals at each other's homes every other day. Towards the end of the holiday, we took the little ones to the matinee of a children's New Year show at school.

There I discovered that it was Olya who had organised for the reporter to send us the photographs. I thanked her publicly, and returned her kiss on the cheek. As we said goodbye and wished one another a happy New Year, Olya and her daughter invited me to stay with them at their house in the mountains for the remainder of the school holidays. I accepted straight away, on condition that my ballerina would teach me to ski, and that there would be no dancing during that period. They agreed, laughing, since there was no room for any kind of dancing around, anyway. Roman leapt in there and then; "Can I come to the country house, too?"

I explained to him it was just a little hut in the middle of the woods, with wolves and bears roaming about outside. "Ah," he pondered. "Perhaps I'd better not, then."

Back home, I told Mother about the photographs and Olya's invitation to stay in the mountains for a few days. She was delighted to hear that I would be having a holiday. The evening before, I packed my rucksack with everything I needed for winter sports and for staying away. To the full bag of pies, Mother added a litre jar of pickle and two little tins of anchovies that my older brother had once thrown out onto the road (although nobody knew about this, except Fedora's family and us). She didn't want me to arrive as an empty-handed guest. At eight the next morning, the chairman himself tapped on the door with his riding crop, and I flew straight out through the gate, looking forward to exciting adventures. In the sledge, as if in a Russian fairy tale illustration, I could make out the figures of three generations of reclining women. Zina and her grandmother under one large sheepskin, Olya under another, turned back ready for the new fellow passenger.

Olya called me and, putting my stuff at the back with the rest of the luggage, I jumped under the sheepskin and was immediately aware of her female warmth. We started immediately. It was a little cold, with a light powdering of snow. Sitting with our backs to the road, we admired the magical winter landscape: the dark green fir trees on the white mountains, the smoking chimneys of awakening villages and playful rays of the pale sun shining between snowflakes. After some zigzagging, a wide frozen lake appeared and, on its shores, the government country houses of the local council management. Around the tall fences of our hut, there were a few scattered firs and a collection of berry bushes. A sizeable villa could be seen in the middle of the little village, which turned out to be the local leisure centre for its holidaying members.

There was a Russian stove at our disposal, on which I immediately secured a space for myself to sleep. Wood was stored under a shelter behind the hut, as well as a little fishing boat. A real toilet was concealed in a corner of the hallway, and there were wide couches large enough for two people in the parlour and the bedroom. The kitchen was fully equipped, and most importantly, the little hut had electricity.

An area large enough for figure skaters had been cleared in the centre of the lake, where they usually gathered after lunch. Zina proposed to teach me to skate, if I was not too afraid of breaking my legs. Hoping to decline this adventure, I quickly pointed out that I had no skates, but in vain. My friend interrupted me and said that, luckily, her mother had skate boots just my size. As a proud Musketeer, I had no option but to agree. Inside, however, I worried. Why did she have to tease me like that? No matter how hard I tried, I always found myself trapped. At that moment we came close to some fishermen on the ice. They were sitting on folding stools or crates for fishing gear and, having lowered live bait through a hole in the ice, were waiting patiently for the silly fish to bite. Some of them had half-empty bottles of vodka next to them.

"Uncle, is that for the fish, too?" I innocently enquired. Zina burst out laughing, while the fisherman scowled at me.

"Get out, boy, before I smash this bottle over your head."

Zina yanked me by the sleeve. "Let's go, you clown! Can't you tell from the bottle that he's drunk?"

For a fearless Musketeer, it was what you could call a strategic retreat. Zina glanced at her mother's watch. "Time to go home. I'm freezing."

"Let me give you a big hug to warm you up," I said, trying to be a gentleman.

"I'm going to give you a hug that'll rattle your ribs in a minute!"

"Rattle my what?" At that moment, my partner grabbed me and held me tight, tripped me up and threw me into a snowdrift. We rolled around in a clinch, sliding along the ice.

"I give in!" I finally screamed, and lay on my back with my arms and legs spread-eagled. The little gypsy sat on my stomach and waved her arms around victoriously, shouting "Hurrah!"

I felt everyone was watching us but there was no one around. My ballerina gave me her hand and, covered in snow, we rushed home across the frozen lake, feeling quite warmed up. Soon afterwards, seeing the figure of another fisherman sitting by a hole in the ice ahead of us, we decided to avoid any possible unpleasantness. But my partner suddenly stopped me.

"Look, he seems dead; you can't see any breath coming out of his nose."

"Don't worry, the old boy probably fell asleep out here in all this fresh air."

I shouted out as I approached the fisherman, but there was no reply. He sat with his elbows on his knees and the fishing rod in his hands. The water in the hole was freezing over. His head had dropped onto his chest, and it was impossible to see whether or not he was breathing. We decided to nudge him. A woman walking past with a bunch of fish asked what we were up to.

"It looks like the old man has frozen to death."

"Dead, is he now? Grinka! Wake up! Deaf as a post, he is."

There was no sound or reply. She came up closer and kicked him in the hip with her boot. He fell off his folding stool on his side, and an empty vodka bottle rolled out from under him. The fisherman bounced up, his eyes wide open and cried, "Have I got a bite?"

We ran home, laughing hysterically all the way. It was so lovely to come into a warm hut after our icy walk. While her father went over to the club to find out about the leisure activities, Olya and her mother set the table and prepared a festive meal. After lunch we decided to take a nap for an hour. Discovering a copy of 'The Count of Monte Cristo' on the bookshelf, I lay reading it for the second time on the warm stove shelf. These four days on the frozen lake went by so quickly that I could not believe it when Olya gently broke the news: "Misha, you're going back to your mummy tonight."

Every morning, we went skiing or sledging; in the afternoon, we had fun at the club. We played mini-billiards, table tennis, quoits and archery. We played like children. Thank God, Olya forbade us from adding skating to our activities, explaining to her daughter that she had no intention of taking home an invalid Musketeer. After dinner, while the adults sat in the club buffet, we watched old silent films in the cinema: Battleship Potemkin, Charlie Chaplin, the circus trainer Durov and other masterpieces of early cinema. I was in seventh heaven and sad to have to leave this corner of paradise. Still, all good things have to come to and end, sooner or later.

On 17th January 1944, we were informed that our father had died. Dusya brought the telegram from the hospital, stating that the patient had died during a violent epileptic fit, after which he failed to regain consciousness. Since we knew that this could happen at any time, the news did not come as a complete surprise, but it was no less emotionally devastating for that. There were no hysterical tears. Mother said nothing. She gripped the back of the chair and stood very still, silently cursing herself for not having been able to see him while he was still alive. Dusya tore her away from the chair, led her to the couch and brought her a glass of water with a tranquiliser. Anna did not touch or react to anything. Three years of searching for a loved one, only to be unable to see him, then losing him again, this time forever. It was cruelly unfair to us children and especially to our mother.

At school, the headmistress took Yosif and me from the last lesson, saying that our mother was ill and needed our help. At first, we were taken aback but, aware of her health problems, we rushed home to help. Dusya met us at the door and told us to wait in the kitchen until Mother, who was in the parlour, felt a little better. When we asked what had happened, she paused.

"Your father passed away, this morning."

She handed Yosif the telegram, which he read and passed to me. I don't know about my brother, but I felt everything inside me being torn to pieces. We both sat there, motionless, staring at the floor. Dusya took off our hats and went back to Mother in the parlour. I can't remember how long we sat there, feeling numb. When the kettle boiled on the primus stove, Dusya came back into the kitchen and prepared us something to eat. She picked up our coats off the floor and told us to go and wash our hands. It was all like a terrifying dream. We could not eat, but had some tea, because our mouths were so dry.

From the parlour, we could hear Dusya begging our mother, "Anna, cry, my dear. Annushka, please try and cry. You'll feel better. After all, Semyon has not totally disappeared from the face of the earth. He lives on in your children. Believe me, your husband's spirit will never leave you."

Mother was obviously not reacting to Dusya's pleas, since the latter came to us, wiping her tears with a handkerchief. "Come in, boys. Perhaps you'll have better luck at comforting her."

Sitting on the couch on either side of her, we took her hands away from her face and pressed them against our chests following the self-same instinct, and without saying anything. She kept staring into the distance, moving her lips silently. We both immediately understood that she was speaking to Daddy, or rather to his spirit, and decided not to interrupt her farewell. We glanced at each other, dropped our heads and pressed Mum's hands against our cheeks. After a while, she took away her hands, hugged us and whispered, "Father is gone. You're orphans, now."

Unable to bear it anymore, we started sobbing. It was Mother's turn to comfort us.

"Never mind, boys, be strong. We have suffered so much during this war. This too, we will survive. The most important, as your father said, is that we stick together."

We decided not to tell Roman anything for the time being, so as not to traumatise him needlessly.

"Why is everyone so silently?" he asked at dinner.

"Silent," corrected the Commander. "All right, why is everyone so silent?"

"Because it's bad for you to talk while you eat," said Yosif, trying to sound clever.

"Why?" Roman kept asking.

Even our upset mother smiled at this. "Yosif is right," she said. We stayed home from school the next day, not wanting to leave Mother alone. We fussed over her all day, helping with house chores, firing the stove and so on. In the afternoon, Dusya came again with a form for claiming our father's pension, since he had died as a result of war injuries. She asked what our plans were, once Odessa had been liberated.

"Whatever happens, the children must complete the academic year here," our Commander replied. "And I also need time to make the necessary arrangements for the District Council to pay for our tickets from Kuybyshev to Odessa, via Kiev."

At the beginning of February, we received a detailed letter from the hospital and all father's documents. They returned our photographs, which they had found under Dad's pillow after he died. He often talked to his companions about us, and kept asking the orderly about his chances of returning to Odessa, to his family. The answers were carefully phrased but nonetheless negative. The shrapnel pieces could not be removed from the brain. The risk of a fatal attack would increase with any worries about his children. The railway from Tashkent to Odessa went through areas that had been destroyed, so it would be a while before regular passenger transport could be resumed. Physically, he was not strong enough to travel unaccompanied, which meant that his chances of seeing his family any time soon were slim. Aware of this, he did not want to make vain promises to his loved one. In the end, his fate was sealed.

In the evening of April 11th 1944, Dusya brought the long-awaited news that Odessa had been freed that day. Our hurrahs were a strange combination of joy and tears. I don't know why people sometimes cry instead of laughing; someone must have got into a muddle when he created human beings. Our loyal protector took a bottle of kvass out of her bag for us men, and a quarter of vodka for the women. We all clinked glasses and drank to victory. The next day, many people congratulated us on the liberation of our home town. The headmistress called my older brother and asked when we were planning to return. When she heard that it would not be before August, she gave a satisfied smile.

The Commander began making arrangements for free tickets from Kuybyshev to Odessa for 1st August. As usual, the school concert was scheduled for the end of June, and the regional inspection for the middle of July.

We hoped that everything would easily fall into the schedule. Just in case, Dusya reserved us a compartment as far as Kiev in the Chairman's name. From there, we would be given seats for Odessa as a matter of course. We were however warned that with so many refugees desperate to return to their homes, there was chaos on the railways. Still, our family was not afraid of the big bad wolf, since we had already gone through the mill; to us, it was no worse than a puppy. Our renewed hope made us blind to any potential risks.

We successfully completed the academic year. My older brother once again confirmed his status as an all-rounder. At the end of season, he organised another tournament for both groups, and received warm thanks for it from the parents. At the post-parents' meeting concert, we reprised our repertoire for the directors' conference in full, which, as a private performance, not many people had seen. The only new dance was the Kazachok that Zina and I performed together, as a gift from me to my partner for her talent and her patience towards me. The audience kept shouting "Encore!" for us to repeat the dance one more time. Zina was truly stunned.

Roman had picked a bunch of wild flowers somewhere and presented it to her after the concert. The ballerina thanked him with a kiss.

"What about me?" I teased her.

"Another time," she snapped back.

"Serves you right," said Roman, turning up his nose at me.

"Look at the lad," I thought. "Barely out of nappies, and already into girls."

As if that were not enough, Olya added fuel to the fire. "Watch out, Musketeer. Your little brother will soon run rings around you!" Everybody was laughing except me. Roman tried to endear himself. "Don't be sad, Misha-Clown, put your thumbs up!"

A few days later, Dusya brought our free train tickets to Odessa, with reserved seats to and from Kiev. She said that the Chairman himself had harangued everyone at the train station until he got what he wanted. On the last Sunday in July, Mother organised a farewell lunch for all those who had in one way or another been a part of our evacuation stay. There were about twenty guests in total. Yosif and I swept the garden thoroughly and arranged the tables and benches, which had been brought from the school. We had enough crockery and cutlery; the problem was filling it all with food and drink. Mother made three huge pots of Ukrainian borscht and baked over a hundred of her famous pies. She prepared herring, olive salad, and aubergine pâté, as though it were a wedding feast in Odessa. The guests brought fruit and drinks, aware of our financial circumstances.

There was a very friendly atmosphere at the lunch, and toast after toast, with many warm congratulations and good wishes. Both chairmen expressed their heartfelt admiration for our mother, who was raising the three of us to be proper men. The headmistress highlighted the enthusiasm of both pupils at her school and wished us luck at our new school in Odessa. The three of them left shortly afterwards, which allowed the other guests to relax without the presence of officials. We, the young generation, sat at a separate table and drank kvass instead of homemade vodka, but made even more noise than the adults, in spite of our alcohol-free drink. The liberation of our home town, as well as our successes in chess and dance were good reasons to celebrate and accounted for our popularity among the other villagers.

In the last two days before our departure, we packed and repacked our rucksacks and bags a dozen times. We returned both bicycles to Old Sidor's relatives, with our deepest thanks. When I said goodbye to Olya's household, I left them our pre-war address in Odessa and promised that, in a year's time, once we were settled, we would invite Mother and daughter to spend the summer holidays in our very own pearl of the Black Sea, Odessa. I had to admit that I could not find the words to express my gratitude for Olya's kindness and my delight in my friendship with Zina and our work together. The three of us found it hard to part. It was equally heart-breaking saying goodbye to Paulya's family – even the goat bleated "Safe journey!" at me. I had become very attached to these simple, kind-hearted people, and would never forget them.

At nine a.m. of the first day in August, the jeep from the Kuybyshev Evacuation Centre arrived to take us to the station. Dusya arrived with it. She locked all the doors and windows, took our keys, and we all sat in silence on the street. We then took it in turns to kiss our protector and started on our journey. We were so upset by this parting that we could not take our eyes off the village that was vanishing in the distance, and where we had left part of our hearts in spite of all our difficulties there. On the other hand, we were returning to our home town, where we knew every cobble on our street, and where we would be welcomed by the waving white branches of flowering acacia trees. Why are people's lives so hard? I thought. Why can't someone just stay in one place, and study, work, play chess and dance? What's the use of moving all the time? Fighting? Running away? Wouldn't life be wonderful if everyone just minded their own business without interfering in other people's? But people are not content with just that. As Nanny Sasha used to say, "People are always getting their arses in a mess and then complaining that life is hard." Strange. The train station had been crowded since early morning. The old jeep driver picked up our heavy bags and began pushing through the crowd towards our carriage, which was reserved for evacuee families. Mother walked behind him, holding Roman by the hand, while Yosif and I were at the tail of the convoy. The driver took us to our compartment, lifted our bags onto the racks and wished us a safe journey. Mother slipped a ten-rouble note into his shirt pocket, and thanked him.

As though following orders, we immediately both took off our rucksacks and pushed them under the racks. We straightened up together, and sat opposite each other. Our movements were completely synchronised, with no prior rehearsal. Once we had finished our study in movement, the four of us breathed a sigh of relief in unison. Then, unable to resist, we all began laughing hysterically. The conductor peeked in, alarmed. "What's the matter?"

Our mother replied, "It's nothing. We're just rehearsing."

He shook his head, sadly. "Poor things, the train hasn't left yet but they've already left their minds behind."

The poor conductor had no way of knowing that this was just a reaction to three years of war.